Struggle and Hope

*Reflections on the recent history
of the Transkeian People*

MDA MDA

ALLAN ZINN (EDITOR)

rapid access publishers

Struggle and Hope - Reflections on the recent history of the Transkeian People

Published by AFRICAN SUN MeDIA under the RAP imprint

First edition 2019

ISBN 978-1-928314-54-7
ISBN 978-1-928314-55-4 (e-book)
https://doi.org/10.18820/9781928314554

Set in Andada 10/15
Cover design, typesetting and production by AFRICAN SUN MeDIA

RAP (Rapid Access Publishers) is a licensed imprint of AFRICAN SUN MeDIA. General works are published under this imprint in print and electronic format.

This publication can be ordered directly from:
www.sun-e-shop.co.za
www.store.it.si (e-books)
africansunmedia.snapplify.com (e-books)
www.africansunmedia.co.za

Contents

Author's note i

About the author i

Preface iii

Introduction 1
Allan Zinn

Chapter 1
Phalo's land 17

Chapter 2
Conquest, colonisation and oppression 23

Chapter 3
AbaThembu – A house divided 29

Chapter 4
Sabata ascends throne 37

Chapter 5
Apartheid machinations 43

Chapter 6
AmaMpondo 47

Chapter 7
The Mpondo succession 53

Chapter 8
The rise of K.D. (Kaiser) Matanzima 55

Chapter 9
Apartheid takes root 65

Chapter 10
The people's response 69

Chapter 11
The Qhitsi revolt 73

Chapter 12
African nationalism and apartheid collide 77

Chapter 13
The Bantustan imbroglio 83

Chapter 14
The Mthentu dispute 87

Chapter 15
AbaThembu are co-opted 91

Chapter 16
Every traditional leader has a price 105

Chapter 17
The Xhosa succession 109

Chapter 18
Ciskei follows Transkei 111

Chapter 19
Matanzima, the autocrat 115

Chapter 20
Greed and graft 125

Chapter 21
The Sabata saga 129

Chapter 22
Coup 147

Chapter 23
King Sabata's reburial 151

Chapter 24
Sebe debacle 155

Chapter 25
AmaMpondomise 161

Chapter 26
Quo Vadis? .... W
171

Postscript 173
Addendum A 179

Author's note

This is a work of non-fiction. I have rendered the events faithfully and truthfully as I recall them or have experienced them or as they were related to me by those who personally witnessed them. Circumstances and conversations depicted in this memoir come from my keen recollection of them and they are told in a way that attempts to evoke the feeling and meaning of what happened and what was said. The views expressed are mine. To anyone who finds the views strong or unacceptable, and to those whose names I did not recall or omitted, I offer sincere apologies.

About the author

Mda Mda is a life-long citizen and resident of the territory that at various times has been known either as Xhosaland, Transkei or (now) the Eastern Cape Province of South Africa. Born in 1923 in the town of Lusikisiki, he was educated at various institutions in and around Transkei, including St John's Practising School in Mthatha, Healdtown near Fort Beaufort and Lovedale College in the town of Alice near King William's Town.

After obtaining his BA degree from the University of Fort Hare in 1943, followed by brief legal studies at the University of Cape Town (UCT) in 1944, he taught English and History at St John's College in Mthatha. In the early 1950s, he commenced his career as a legal practitioner. After some 50-odd years, he retired as a practising attorney in 2004. In 2015, he was awarded the President of Convocation Medal from UCT for his "contribution to the common good".

As a member of the Non-European Unity Movement (NEUM) and various community-based organisations, including, being General Secretary of the Transkei Organised Bodies (affiliated to the All African Convention), Mda was an active campaigner against the iniquitous apartheid system. Today, he is life member of NEUM's successor, the New Unity Movement. Well into his 90s, he continues to enjoy good health, and as his memoir attests, retains a sharp mental acuity. He lives on a small property in Viedjesville, 22 km outside Mthatha, which he shares with his daughter, Thandeka.

The Editor, Allan Zinn and Author, Mda Mda meet at eldest daughter, Thobeka Mda's flat in Kenilworth, Cape Town, December 2018*

* Photo taken by Charles Thomas, Cape Town researcher, whom we wish to thank for his role in the successful completion of the book project.

Preface

In telling the story of our[1] reaction to conquest, resistance to oppression and struggle for liberation, I have concentrated on the Eastern Cape, in particular the Transkei. That is the region in the south-east of the sub-continent, extending from the Kei River to the Mtamvuna River on the border with KwaZulu Natal. The British invaders or colonisers called the area Transkei and allowed it to remain under indigenous occupation as the biggest "native reserve" in South Africa.

In their northward push from the Western Cape, the British had already gobbled up a big bulk of Xhosaland from the Gamtoos River Valley right up to the Kei River. In the process, Xhosaland had been wiped off the face of the map and, for colossal cheek, the heart of Xhosaland had been named British Kaffraria.

With the formation of the Union of South Africa in 1910, British imperialism gave the local Whites a large share in the running of the country. The Black majority, although British subjects in name, had no rights and were left under the power and control of the White population. The pretext and subterfuge for Black subjugation was that the Blacks were uneducated savages and "heathens". However, a door was open for assimilation of "civilised natives". There were even advocates of "equal rights for all civilised persons".

During the Second World War, South Africa's Prime Minister, Field Marshall J.C. Smuts, in fending off agitation and rising calls for human rights for the Black population of the country, made an important policy statement in which he declared that "Segregation ha[d] fallen on evil days". However, there was no action on the part of the government to complement those words. His ever-ready excuse was the heavy burden of the war effort. Things would surely come right after the defeat of Hitler.

The National Party (NP), though, was making different noises.

It was wrong and dangerous, the NP maintained, to give the Natives promises of citizenship. The "trouble" in the country was caused by educated Natives who thought they were equal to Whites. South Africa was a White man's country and the Native a servant with no rights. As if to show that segregation was here to stay,

---

[1] The author explains that "our" refers to the indigenous people conquered by the European invaders.

Mr Harry Lawrence, a Minister in Smuts's wartime cabinet, had a law passed creating a "Coloured Affairs Department" and a "Coloured Advisory Council". Those designated "Coloured" were up in arms.

For the first time in South Africa, there was strong and determined opposition to the government. The Coloured[2] community saw Lawrence's move as the first step in a sinister move to elbow them out of the body politic. They equated this to what had been done in 1936 by the Hertzog-bills which disenfranchised the Africans. There was enlightened leadership which mobilised the Coloured community and all organisations to fight this encroachment on their rights. Political organisations and civil structures were brought together under a federal body called the Anti-Coloured Affairs Department (Anti-CAD).

The Anti-CAD was fighting all discrimination and all segregated bodies, including the Natives Representative Council in Pretoria. They were spreading their campaign to include all the oppressed. Inevitably, this led to the formation in 1943 of the NEUM or "Unity Movement". This was a call across race, colour or creed for the building of a nation in a non-racial democratic South Africa. There was no bargaining and the Ten Point Programme of the Unity Movement provided the *sine qua non* for a new nation. This was to be copied 12 years later by the Congress Movement with its Freedom Charter.

In 1948, it was D.F. Malan's NPthat was to win elections for the all-White National Assembly. It won on an apartheid ticket. The success of the NP, with its neo-Nazi apartheid policy, was to be the dominant factor in South African politics for years to come. This was to test to the limit the strength and resilience of those striving for change and for a democratic order in a single South African nation.

The idea of the country being populated by numerous "nations" would be unproblematic if one were referring to pre-colonial South Africa, where "nation" was generally taken to refer to distinct population groupings, such as "The Xhosa Nation" and "The Zulu Nation", which were largely autonomous tribal groupings with cultural and linguistic affinities. Post-1910 (that is, after the formation of the Union of South Africa), when it became clear that imperialist capitalism was

---

2   According to Encyclopaedia Brittanca (website: https://www.britannica.com/topic/
     Coloured [Accessed 12 January 2019]) "Coloured, formerly Cape Coloured, a person of
     mixed European ("white") and African ("black") or Asian ancestry, as officially defined by
     the South African government from 1950-1991." From the outset, there was (and continues
     to be) a strenuous rejection – particularly, but not exclusively – in left wing circles of identity
     politics in general, and the labelling of people or groups as "Coloured" in particular. The
     application of ascriptive labels of this kind is seen as a form of racism, and in South Africa,
     there is a rich history of struggle against it.

consolidating the state, to better to exploit its largely indigenous working class, and, in the process, to exclude that working class from full citizenship, the struggle for a single, non-racial democratic South Africa was mobilised. However, this did not automatically lead to the dismantling of tribal identities, which continued to be fundamental, defining markers in society. Thus, through much of the 20th century, people saw themselves not merely as workers, men, or Christians or whatever, but as Xhosa (or Zulu or Sotho) workers, men, Christians, etc. In an era when discrimination was based on "race", it is not difficult to see how this would play into the hands of the oppressors – if you uncritically accept yourself as this or that race or nation, you inadvertently create a basis for me to exploit you. Indeed, terms like "racial capital" (that is, the enrolment by capital of racial identities in the project of capitalist class exploitation) have arisen to reflect how race (at least in the context of South Africa) intermediates class exploitation.

As much of the drama of this narrative unfolds in an era when "race/nation" – and, importantly, the institutions (such as chieftainship) which underpin it – was the dominant paradigm, the author has chosen to locate the discussion within such paradigm.

The Transkei was peopled by several "nations" who by-and-large had not engaged the invaders/colonisers in the fight in defence of the fatherland.

It was the indomitable Xhosa warriors who had salvaged African pride and honour with their dogged resistance against heavy odds. That they were able to accomplish so much while having to fend off back-stabbing by amaMfengu is amazing. Unluckily, until the end, amaMfengu were caught on the wrong side of history. (However, I want to believe that the day is still coming when they will make amends.)

AbaThembu did not distinguish themselves during this period either and, in fact, have very little to be proud of. They had even come to be regarded to be as pliant as amaMfengu and placed in the category of "good and dependable Natives".

However, during resistance to apartheid, abaThembu were to shine and take on a new profile. If they produced the chief villain in Kaiser Daliwonga ("K.D.") Matanzima, they also scored with the king hero, Sabata Dalindyebo and countless numbers of unnamed heroines and heroes.

There were also the amaMpondo, who hitherto had had an ambiguous record. Beneath their youthful and carefree exterior, the amaMpondo concealed a depth of sagacity and hardiness. Their readiness to play the fool hid their true strength and worldly wisdom. While the Thembu resistance was a long and drawn out affair, the

Mpondo peasant revolt was a giant wave and irresistible, like a tsunami. It was also a heady and thrilling experience and did much to raise their reputation. Although it was short-lived, its results were not. Things could never be the same as before.

The ascendancy of rabid Afrikaner nationalism and its neo-Nazi apartheid policy was the harbinger of strife and turmoil in the country. We (the political activists imbued with the ideas of the Unity Movement) were already in the field and had cut our political teeth by siding with the peasants in their opposition to unpopular measures such as the Rehabilitation Scheme of 1944, about which Lungisile Ntsebeza has the following to say:

> As early as the 1920s, the effects of overcrowding and overstocking arising
> out of restricting [B]lack Africans to Reserves totaling less than ten percent
> of the South African land surface were beginning to manifest themselves.
> This was mainly in the form of soil erosion. [3]

And so, to solve the problem, the government did not move to increase the allocation of land to the reserves, but instead introduced its *Betterment* or *Rehabilitation* policy, which involved "fencing, resettlements and stock limitation". [4]

The infamous Rehabilitation Scheme was central in precipitating the mass protests which engulfed South Africa in the middle years of the last century.

We, the young activists, belonged to the Transkei Voters' Association, Cape African Teachers' Association (CATA) and the Transkei Organised Bodies – all affiliated to the African Convention. This brought us under the NEUM, with its Ten Point Programme as the basic minimum acceptable set of demands in the fight for full citizenship rights, and a new South African nation, free of any discrimination on the grounds of race, religion, colour, creed or sex. (The Unity Movement was the first organisation to formulate a coherent programme of political demands – its Ten Point Programme, which demands full political rights for all, and which also calls for a fundamental resolution to the problem of the grossly inequitable land ownership and usage rights in South Africa.)[5]

Hitherto, educated Africans deferred to and relied on White political leadership. It was the likes of Mrs Margaret Ballinger, Advocate D.B. Molteno, Senator Edgar Brookes and Hyman Basner who held sway. As youth, we were rebels. We were

---

[3] Kepe, T. & Ntsebeza, L .(eds.). 2012. *Rural Resistance in South Africa: The Mpondo Revolts after Fifty Years.* Cape Town: UCT Press. 24.

[4] Ibid.

[5] Note from the APDUSA website: http://www.apdusa.org.za/book-authors/tabata-i-b/ [Accessed 11 January 2019].

attracted by the radical and uncompromising stand of the Unity Movement, for full equality and rejection of White Supremacy. Political leaders in the Transkei, on the other hand, were members of the Natives Representative Council and also seniors in the Bhunga, the United Transkeian Territories General Council (UTTGC). The big names were Mr C.K. Sakwe, Mr Elijah Qamata, Mr Saul Mabhude, Mr W.W. Dana and other Bhunga stalwarts.

While the elders admired our indefatigable zeal and earnestness, they decried what they perceived to be our impetuosity, inexperience, foolhardiness and extremism. It was the rural folk, the peasants and the uneducated (the *Reds*) who found our views in harmony with theirs. It was to be an ongoing battle for turf as we tried to align Transkei residents with the policy of the Unity Movement. The boycott weapon and the policy of non-collaboration were useful tools in our armoury. This found ready acceptance from the peasants.

It is nevertheless a painful historical truth that Transkei carries the burden of shame of being the place where the apartheid government had its first success in creating a puppet Bantustan homeland. Undeniably, the Transkei Bantustan government was the pride of apartheid, for its abject and unquestioning subservience to its masters in Pretoria.

The rulers' audacious Homelands policy, which sought to carve South Africa up into a number of "independent" or "semi-independent" Bantustans, relied on the willing participation of key members of the caste of chiefs and the intelligentsia to make it work. Collaborator in-chief (no pun intended!) was K.D. Matanzima, who was to become the first president of an independent Transkei. He wasted no time in using his new-found status not only to strengthen his grip on power, but also to settle scores.

The rise and climb of Chief K.D. Matanzima was phenomenal and the marginalisation and eventual elimination of the Thembu sovereign, King Sabata Dalindyebo, a great tragedy. The two events epitomise the victory of the apartheid government and the trouncing of the opposing democratic forces. As the story unfolds, the ruthlessness, single-mindedness of purpose, cynical contempt for all civilised norms, unbridled use of force and naked dictatorship, are all revealed in their ugliness. This was used as a means to force down the throats of unwilling and resisting people, the dictates of depraved racial supremacists.

At this juncture, it is apposite to make an explanation, as well as an apology for the many gaping holes and glaring omissions in this memoir. There is not the slightest mention of amaXesibe. This unintended slight seems to imply they made no contribution and did not participate in the liberation struggle. Far from it! There are other nations who can justly claim that they have also been overlooked. The story herein is not exhaustive: it is in the nature of a synopsis. Perhaps it will be possible in a later edition, time and circumstances permitting, to make the necessary inclusions and additions. That would make the book more balanced.

It is unfair to praise and glorify some at the exclusion of others. The glorious story of the bravery of common people and the readiness to sacrifice all in the cause of liberty belongs to all. It is not the preserve of a few. I have been astounded to find that every community, every clan, every tribe, every nation and every section of the people has members who answered the call of duty and who stood up to be counted.

It is apartheid that was the fount of evil.

With all his evil deeds, Chief K.D. Matanzima was not a bad man spoiling a good thing. The sin of the Matanzimas, the Patrick Mphephus (Venda), the Cedric Phathudis (Lebowa), the Lucas Mangopes (Bophuthatswana), the Lennox Sebes (Ciskei) and the Hudson Ntsanwisis (Gazankulu) et al., was to sell themselves, body and soul, to work the evil system through their willingness to lie and deceive on their masters' behalf.

Introduction

ALLAN ZINN

In his opening chapter entitled, "Phalo's land," author Mda Mda tells us that "Before conquest and colonisation, a striking feature of the [Transkeian] territory was its verdant pastures and vast herds of cattle and goats." He adds, "Small wonder the country's inhabitants were proud and successful livestock farmers. Grain production, primarily maize and sorghum, made the territory self-sufficient. The people were prosperous, well nourished, healthy and robust."

Fast-forward to mid-twentieth century Transkei, and we have this depressing observation by the leader of the All African Convention (AAC), Isaac Tabata in 1945:

> Today our people are disease-ridden because of malnutrition; they haven't the oxen to plough; the majority of the babies do not survive the first year because mothers are too starved to be able to feed them. Children are dying like flies from all sorts of diseases because there isn't enough cow's milk to build up their resistance to disease. These well-known facts give the lie direct to the statement that the Africans keep too many cattle. On the contrary, they have far too few cattle for their requirements. It is not that the cattle are too many, but that the land is too small. There is an appalling shortage of land.[6]

Such was the result of the government's "Native Policy," part of the ongoing process of dispossession – of primitive capital accumulation – the continuities of which are all too evident in today's South Africa, all these years later.

---

[6] Quoted from Tababta, I.B. 1945. *The Rehabilitation Scheme A New Fraud*. Online: http://www.apdusa.org.za/wp-content/books/rehabscheme.pdf [Accessed 18 November 2018].

Today – some 20-odd years after the "miracle" of 1994, "Phalo's land"[7] has been incorporated into an expanded territory called the "Eastern Cape Province." Have things changed since Tabata's 1945? Certainly not for the better, if Kate Wilkinson is to be believed. According to her article *FACTSHEET: South Africa's official poverty numbers*,[8] in 2015, "over half of South Africa's population (55,5%) lives in poverty. However, there are certain groups which are more vulnerable to poverty ... the Eastern Cape had the highest share of poor residents at 72,9%."

So: is there cause for hope, as suggested in Mda Mda's title to this volume? *Most certainly!* the author would no doubt exclaim – but not without prior and relentless struggle. Colonial exploitation morphed into apartheid exploitation, which in turn has morphed into neoliberal exploitation. The legacy of capitalist class domination, in all its transformations, persists.

Pre-colonial times

Pre-colonial times were, of course, pre-capitalist times; some 150 years of capitalism have broken and distorted, but not obliterated many key features of African social life which existed prior to colonisation.

At the time of colonial contact, most African societies in the Cape were organised into semi-autonomous chiefdoms which were separated from each other by "poorly defined or non-existent" boundaries. In areas where the chiefdom consisted of a cluster of chieftaincies, a king or a senior chief would become the head of the chiefdom. The lineage was the unit of society "which had its territorial base in the homestead." Lineages were traced through the descendants of male ancestors and tended "to segment," with men hiving off to form their own lineages. Only male descendants could be heirs. The position of a king or senior chief was hereditary and was never decided democratically by the subjects.[9]

---

[7] The Mnquma Local Municipality says of Phalo: "Great King Phalo [was] the Absolute Ruler of [the] Xhosa nation. Phalo reigned from 1700-1775 and is deeply etched in the memories of the Xhosa people for uplifting his nation by consolidating and strengthening their authority and power over other South African nations. King Phalo is also remembered for establishing the identity and values of the Xhosa nation. He was buried in Tongwana Administrative Area in Butterworth." Onllne: http://www.mnquma.gov.za/Content.aspx?pageID=136 [Accessed 18 November 2018].

[8] Her article, published on 15 February 2018. Online: https://africacheck.org/factsheets/factsheet-south-africas-official-poverty-numbers/ [Accessed 18 November 2018].

[9] Thanks to Fani Ncapayi, from whose 2013 doctoral thesis these points were drawn.

The king and chief operated through a male-dominated structure of councillors who acted as their advisers. Thus, women were not part of the chiefdom's council. Councillors were not necessarily of "royal blood," but were chosen on the basis of their experience and skills. Although the king could not interfere in the political affairs of other chieftaincies, he still had overall authority over issues of custom, and junior chiefs consulted him about certain rituals and the resolution of disputes among them. This therefore, elevated the king to the status of a father figure in the chiefdom.

Because the chiefdom was polygamous, it had more than one homestead to accommodate each wife, who lived in her own homestead. Mature sons of the king were encouraged to establish their own chieftaincies, sometimes as junior chiefs within the jurisdiction of the chiefdom.

The king, who was the chiefdom's political head, performed various roles that included executive, military, judicial and religious duties. As an executive, the king sat in on community meetings, listening to the views of his subjects. He also handled disputes among the junior chiefs and made decisions about security and the army of the chiefdom.

Although there was no democracy in the choice of who became king, as the position was hereditary, there was an element of democracy in how decisions on governance matters were reached. Decisions were based on consultation, discussion and consensus.

In traditional society the African chief normally held the land on behalf of his people. He had the power to allocate arable land for use but never outright ownership. Grazing land was held in common, but the chief could control access to it by the villagers' livestock (Davenport, 1991:164).[10]

The Colonial Era – building the structures of exploitation

In the larger scheme of things, Transkei – like all parts of South and southern Africa – was drawn inexorably into the burgeoning vortex of industrial capitalism that was driving the historical transformation of the sub-continent from the mid-to-late 1800s. The needs of the mining industry – the gold-mining industry in particular – were shaping the pattern of social relations moving forward from around the end of the nineteenth-century. Key features in the unfolding socio-economic landscape included the following:

---

[10]   This point appears in Ncapayi's thesis as a direct quotation from Davenport, T.R.H. 1991. *South Africa. A modern history.* 4th Edition. Braamfontein: Macmillan.

Enclavity: South Africa's economy was established principally as an "enclave economy," the main purpose of which was to channel mineral and other resources to the British imperialist centre. Guy Mhone tells that colonisation had led to the establishment of an economy in terms of which the capitalist sector "was grafted onto pre-capitalist forms of production."[11] Thus, from the very beginning the South African economy was not developed in response to the needs of the country's inhabitants as a whole, but fitted as an appendage to the requirements of the British Empire. This has sometimes led to economies such as South Africa's being described as "dual," to mean it consisted of a modern sector existing side-by-side (and feeding off) a traditional or rural sector.

Cheap Labour: In a detailed analysis, Frederick Johnstone[12] outlines the imperatives of the gold mining industry and their concomitant social impacts.

- The viability of the gold mining industry was critically dependent on ongoing flows of ultra-cheap, ultra-exploitable[13] labour supplies, without which there would have been no gold mining industry, since its costs would have proven too prohibitive.
- The sources of this "ultra-cheap, ultra-exploitable" labour were largely the local, indigenous population groupings, including the communities of the Transkei.
- In order to secure the ultra-cheapness and ultra-exploitability of labour, the industry had necessarily to resort to extra-economic coercion, including a battery of legislative and administrative provisions that translated as what Johnstone called "exploitation colour bars" and "job colour bars." Given the rulers' dominant power, the system was underwritten by naked force – how else would the industry have pried the people off the land and into virtual slavery?
- *Semi-proletarianisation.* What partially enabled the mines to pay wages below the "minimum-acceptable-wage"[14] threshold for the reproduction of the workers' basic needs was the existence of the rural support structure. This meant that the mass of mine workers remained dependent on or tied to the rural economy for their subsistence, just as the rural economy came to depend on the cash-flows from migrant workers to their families back home.[15] Neville Alexander quotes from a Chamber of Mines statement in 1943:

---

[11] Mhone, G. 2000. Enclavity and Constrained Labour Absorptive Capacity in Southern African Economies. ILO/SAMAT Discussion Paper No 12. International Labour Organization Southern Africa Multidisciplinary Advisory Team (Ilo/Samat) Harare, Zimbabwe.

[12] Johnstone, F.A.1976. *Class, race and gold: A study of class relations and racial discrimination in South Africa.* London: Routledge & Kegan Paul.

[13] Ibid. (These are terms which Johnstone uses throughout his book.)

[14] See Wallerstein I. 2003. *Historical Capitalism.* Kindle Location 262. London: Verso.

[15] Ibid.

The ability of the mines to maintain their native labour force by means of tribal natives from the Reserves at rates of pay which are adequate for this migratory class of native but inadequate for the detribalised native is a fundamental factor in the economy of the gold mining industry. (p. 61)[16]

(Racial) segregation and oppression. With respect to the Compound system (in terms of which Black workers were housed in men-only barrack-like structures). Not only were the compounds divided along tribal lines, but separated the workers from their White counterparts, thus, "deepening the gulf between skilled and unskilled workers, and further reducing the likelihood of a class-based form of organisation and action."[17]

Much of ruling class colonial policy in the first part of the twentieth-century was driven by the Glen Grey Act of 1894. The Act was passed by the parliament of the Cape Colony, whose prime minister at the time was Cecil John Rhodes. It established a system of individual (rather than communal) land tenure, and created a labour tax to force Xhosa men into employment on commercial farms and in industry. (The act was so named because, although it was later extended to a larger area, it initially applied only in the Glen Grey district. Glen Grey is a former name for the area around Lady Frere, east of Queenstown, in the Eastern Cape province of South Africa.)[18]

In the words of W.P. van Schoor, the Act's "aim was the destruction of the African peasant, to deprive him of land and cattle and to smoke him out to the mines to work."[19]

The Act also had widespread governance implications. The Cape Colony's voters' roll was "non-racial," but limited the political power of voters of non-European origin by educational and property qualifications. Since the Act would have raised the number of non-Europeans who would meet the property qualification, a special provision in the Act prohibited this from happening. Individuals who under the Act had become land owners were expressly excluded by the Act from qualifying thereby to vote in the Cape parliament – a further expression of the cynicism of the non-racialism practiced by Cape Liberalism.

---

[16]   Alexander, N. (writing as No Sizwe) 1979. (digital edition 2013) *One Azania, One Nation. The national question in South Africa.* London: Zed Press.

[17]   Delius, P. 2017. The History of Migrant Labor in South Africa (1800-2014). Online: https://bit.ly/2JacJQF [Accessed 12 December 2018].

[18]   From South African History Online. Glen Grey Division. Online: https://www.sahistory.org.za/places/glen-grey-division [Accessed 13 December 2018].

[19]   Article by Van Schoor, W.P. 1951. The Origin and Development of Segregation in South Africa. A.J. Abrahamse Memorial Lecture. Cumberwood: APDUSA Views.

In addition, the Act also dealt with Native local self-government and the setting up of district councils. In 1898, provisions of the Act relating to individual land tenure and local self-government were applied to the Transkeian Territories. (This system was replaced in 1955 by the Bantu Authorities Acts.)

A big part of the legitimisation myth that British colonialism came clothed in was their supposed "civilizing mission" – the "rationale for colonisation purporting to contribute to the spread of civilization and used mostly in relation to the Westernization of indigenous peoples" (Wikipedia, 12 December 2018). It reflects the arrogance of the conqueror, implying as it does that assimilating *them* into *ours* is a higher purpose. Pierre-Andre Tadieuff in his *The Force of Prejudice*,[20] refers to this process as "solidarities of reason," whereby racist assimilation, which is associated with imperialism – "imperialist assimilation" – results in a colonised people being forcibly integrated into the culture and norms of the dominating country. (p. 304).

In the case of South Africa, the Christian Missionary Movement played a pre-eminent role.[21] A major part of its legacy was the spawning of an educated elite during the colonial era. As Timothy Gibbs put it:

> *African nationalism ... was fabricated by the mission school educated elites who emerged in the wake of colonial conquest. These elites were particularly prominent in parts of the Transkei and the Eastern Cape where wealthy groups of independent African traders and farmers often prospered in the backwash of colonial conquest and the frontier wars.[22]*

Transkei and the Eastern Cape had the "densest concentration"[23] of mission schools in South Africa – Methodists, Anglicans, Catholics: all vied for influence.

- For a brief historical moment, the (liberal) Cape Colony's 1853 constitution permitted *all men regardless of race* to vote – provided they met specified property and educational qualifications. The moment there was a rise in the number of voters of African descent, the qualifications were raised to ensure that White legislative power was not threatened. Initially, the educated elite was seduced into believing that the rights accompanying their "earned" civilization were immutable, but there was a rude awakening in store, as the following brief chronology of events shows:

---

20 Taguieff, P-A. (Trans. Melehy, H.) 2001. *The Force of Prejudice: On Racism and Its Doubles.* Minneapolis: University of Minnesota Press.

21 See Taylor, D. 1952. *The Role of the Missionaries in Conquest. Unity Movement History Series.* Cumberwood: APDUSA.

22 Gibbs, T. 2014. *Mandela's Kinsmen: Nationalist Elites & Apartheid's First Bantustan.* Johannesburg: Jacana Media (Pty) Ltd.

23 Ibid.

- The "colour blind" franchise was introduced in 1853. Sir Harry Smith Porter, Attorney General of the Cape Colony had recommended that voting rights be restricted to "the more intelligent and industrious men of colour." The strategy was clearly to hide the real inequalities in Cape Colonial society under a franchise law whose terms seemed to apply to all equally, irrespective of colour. This was the strategy of the qualified franchise. All would-be voters had to have a minimum of schooling and had to own property valued at a minimum of £25. These qualifications, of course, disfranchised the over-whelming majority, that is, those not of "European descent". As was the intention.[24]
- Even this limited, "harmless" concession to the "civilized natives" was eroded in 1887 by the Parliamentary Registration Act which, "without any reference whatever to colour, stated that 'no person shall be entitled to be registered as a voter by reason of his sharing in any communal or tribal occupation of lands or building.' And thereby struck some 30 000 Africans from the voters roll."[25]
- Then, in 1892, the Franchise Act raised the property qualification from £25-£75, thereby decreasing – by the time of the 1893 registration of voters – the Non-European voters by 3 848 and increasing the White voters by 4 306. This decrease and increase respectively occurred despite the "compromise" that voters already on the roll should remain there.[26]

The South Africa Act of 1909 placed control and administration of 'Native Affairs' under the Governor-General. The primary concern of government was to prevent any revival of the military power of the African chiefdoms, whose resistance to White encroachment and settlement had only relatively recently been broken. (The Ninth and last) Frontier War was waged against the Xhosa in 1878.)[27]

Accordingly, where chiefdoms survived as territorially based corporate entities, overwhelmingly in those areas which after passage of the Native Land Act of 1913 were designated 'Native Areas,' official policy was designed to bypass and weaken the chiefs. A system of direct rule was imposed upon the formerly autonomous chiefdoms, the legitimacy of chiefs was deliberately undermined, and subaltern authority was widely – if not uniformly – devolved upon headmen.[28]

24 Mokone, S. 1977. Majority Rule – Some Notes. Cape Town: Teachers' League of South Africa.

25 Ibid.

26 Ibid.

27 Bank, L. & Southall, R. Traditional Leaders in South Africa's New Democracy. *The Journal of Legal Pluralism and Unofficial Law*. 28(37-38):407-430. https://doi.org/10.1080/07329113.1996.10756489

28 Ibid.

This model had earlier been developed in the Transkei, the whole of which by 1894 had become subject to the Cape Government, which had wrought a fundamental political change, as described by Hammond-Tooke (as quoted in Bank and Southall):[29]

> *No longer were the grass-covered plains and mountain uplands the inalienable territory of small, autonomous chiefdoms ... By a stroke of the pen political structures had been suddenly widened and the chiefdoms transformed into units of local government ...*

This was effected by introducing an administrative system that cut across tribal boundaries. A grid of twenty-seven magisterial districts, that paid scant regard to the old political units, was imposed on the tribal pattern. The districts themselves were subdivided into locations, approximately thirty to a district, and over each was placed a headman, appointed to the post by the administration. Although, in fact, succession to office was almost invariably inherited, in law the headman was appointed by Government and was subject to bureaucratic rules of censure and dismissal. The chiefs, as such, were all but ignored.[30]

The main reduction of authority was in the judicial sphere. No chief or headman was permitted to decide any criminal case and even in civil cases their role was merely one of arbitration. They had no power to enforce their decisions and any litigant not satisfied with these decisions could bring his case to the magisterial court where it was heard *de novo*.[31]

The role of the chiefs was further undermined by the 1927 Native Administration Act[32] which, inter alia gave the Governor-General systematic powers to appoint, recognize and remove chiefs, and to compel their service as administrative functionaries. Such political subordination led to the transformation of the African peoples of South Africa from "self-sufficient and autonomous chiefdoms" into either communities of peasants, living on attenuated tribal lands which became increasingly dependent upon the export of migrant labour, or wage labourers who worked for firms and farms and lived in areas owned by whites.[33]

---

[29] Ibid.

[30] Ibid.

[31] Ibid.

[32] The Act – variously known as the "Native"/"Bantu"/"Black" Administration Act of 1927 – "set up a separate legal system for the administration of African law and made the proclaimed Black areas subject to a separate political regime from the remainder of the country, ultimately subject only to rule by proclamation, not parliament." Online: https://en.wikipedia.org/wiki/Native_Administration_Act,_1927 [Accessed 15 December 2018].

[33] Bank & Southall, op. cit.

In 1930, the district councils were amalgamated into the United Transkeian Territories General Council (UTTGC) which consisted of twenty-six district magistrates, three councillors from each district, and three chiefs (in an *ex-officio* capacity). The UTTGC was essentially a dummy body, controlled by the magistrates and the Native Affairs department.

A few short years later, in 1936, "dummyism" was reinforced by the establishment of the Native Representative Council, in terms of which the highly-qualified, token "non-racial vote" in the Cape Province was discontinued. As Wikipedia put it:

> *With this act, the small black elite – most blacks never had the vote – were removed from the common rolls on which they had been able to register since 1854. Chiefs, local councils, urban advisory boards and election committees in all provinces were to elect four whites to the senate by a system of block voting. The act also created a Native Representative Council of six white officials, four nominated and twelve elected Africans.*[34]

Colonial exploitation of the country was proceeding apace. In the year prior to the Nationalist victory at the Whites-only polls, the ruling class unveiled its Rehabilitation (also known as "Betterment") Scheme in Butterworth in 1947. Perhaps Isaac Tabata contextualises it best when he says:

> *To understand this Rehabilitation Scheme we must see it as something which will complete the exploitation of the Black man. We must see it fitting into and following upon all the laws already passed against the African peasant. At the same time we must see it as a link in the long chain of oppression affecting the whole African population. It flows directly from the basic policy of the country, known as the "Native Policy". And if we understand this "Native Policy" then we shall be in a position to understand not only the meaning of the Rehabilitation Schemes but also all other measures passed against the Black man.*[35]

The effect of the 1913 Land Act led inevitably to (massive) overcrowding in the Reserves, with devastating effects on the lives of the people. The government's solution included stock culling (of cattle, sheep, goats and even donkeys), fencing off of free-range grazing land, and "villagisation" (that is, forced removals which broke up established communities).[36] Needless to say, this put the government on a collision

---

[34] Wikipedia, op. cit.

[35] Tabata, op. cit.

[36] Reddings, S. 2006. *Sorcery and Sovereignty: Taxation, Power, and Rebellion in South Africa, (1880-1963)*. Ohio: Ohio University Press.

course with the people, whose lives and livelihoods were further jeopardised by these "solutions." Tabata powerfully voiced the opposition to the government's measures: "It is not that the cattle are too many, but that the land is too small. There is an appalling shortage of land."[37]

According to Colin Bundy, "One of the most immediate effects of the stock-culling and rehabilitation issues was a deepening of hostility towards chiefs, headmen, district councillors and *Bungha*[38] spokesmen. Local popular associations opposed to councillors and chiefs sprang up in several districts between 1945 and 1948."[39]

This opposition to chiefs as a collaborationist layer carried over into the era of Nationalist government rule after 1948, as chiefs were seen as the "extended arm of the apartheid regime." (Ntsebeza, p. 29).

The Apartheid Era – The Bantuisation of society

The Bantu Authorities Act in 1951 led to the creation of ten Bantustans (or "homelands" as the rulers would have preferred to call them). Bantustan policy was a key pillar in the racial-capitalist project of controlling the supply of cheap labour to and from the industrial centres of the country. In terms of its provisions, racio-ethnic classifications were used effectively to deprive Black South African citizens of their citizenship rights by condemning them to citizenship of the homeland corresponding to their "racial" or "ethnic" or "tribal" classification. Thus, Transkei for the Xhosa, Kwazulu for the Zulu, and so on.

The Act's roots lay in the colonial-era legislation which was established to consolidate nineteenth-century colonial dispossession of the indigenous people (that is, the process of primitive capital accumulation) and 20th century segregation of society along racial lines. The principal pieces of colonial-era legislation included the 1927 Native Administration Act and later the 1936 Native Trust and Land Act. The 1927 Act codified customary law, giving chiefs greater power over their subjects, and the 1936 Act sought to make the Reserves economically and agriculturally more viable by expanding some Reserve land but also by minimizing African political rights outside of Reserve territory.[40]

---

37 Tabata, op. cit.

38 The spelling varies – Bunga, Bhunga, Bungha are all common variants.

39 Bundy, C. 1984. Land and Liberation: The South African National Liberation Movement and the Agrarian Question, 1920s-1960s. *African Review of Political Economy*, July.

40 Phillips, L. 2017. History of South Africa's Bantustans Subject: Political History, Social History, Southern Africa. https://doi.org/10.1093/acrefore/9780190277734.013.80

But the Bantu Authorities Act's immediate and key purpose was to licence the rulers to clear surplus-to-requirements workers from the centres of production. As Laura Phillips tells us:

> *Large numbers of African tenants were moved from farms and dumped into the territories that would become the Bantustans. African communities were also forcibly removed from what were officially termed "black spots," freehold land owned by Africans in white-designated areas.*[41]

In addition, it was estimated that by the early 1980s, about six hundred thousand people were forced from black spots into the Bantustans, and that the African population on farmlands dropped from thirty-four percent in 1951; to 31,3 % in 1960; and 20,6 % in 1980.[42]

Ruling class strategy for implementing Bantu Authorities in the Reserves was via a process of indirect rule, with chiefs and headmen co-opted into the machinery of government. This was to prefigure the maturation of the policy of Grand Apartheid, in terms of which the relevant bodies (Tribal, Regional and Territorial Authorities) would become the basis of the Bantustan administration system, come "independence."

Allison Drew provides a nice summary of how Bantu Authorities worked:

> *Premised on the retribalization of rural Africans, which was to serve as the basis for their political representation, Bantu Authorities had a pyramidal structure. At the base were Tribal Authorities, composed of chiefs and headmen. Over these were District Authorities, then Regional Authorities, Paramount Chiefs, and finally Territorial Authorities, composed of all members of all Regional Authorities and which nominated a head approved by the South African President. Territorial Authorities were given expanded powers to serve as the basis for eventual independence.*[43]

Drew adds that "chiefs became the pivotal intermediaries by which government was to obtain African acquiescence. (p. 72). She goes on to quote Govan Mbeki (from his *The Peasants' Revolt*):

> *[T]hough the whip has remained in the hand of the White government, it has been the Chiefs, the new jockeys, riding the reserve horse, who have applied the spurs. The Chiefs are now well in the saddle, supported by the*

---

41   Ibid.

42   Ibid.

43   Drew, A. 2012. Govan Mbeki's: The Peasants' Revolt. In: T. Kepe & L. Ntsebeza (eds.). *Rural Resistance in South Africa: The Mpondo Revolts after Fifty Years.* Cape Town: UCT Press.

> *headmen who represent them in the villages. This explains the intense*
> *resistance across the reserves against Bantu Authorities and the chiefs who*
> *collaborated with it." (p. 73)[44]*

Given their role as labour-feeders to the White capitalist economy, the Bantustans were necessarily kept in a state of semi-to-grinding poverty so that they would not develop independent (and possibly, competitive) "national" economies. This did not prevent them from growing sizeable middle-classes. Especially from the 1970s onwards, as the ranks of the class of traditional leaders was swelled by the growing numbers of professionals (doctors, lawyers), small business operators, civil servants (teachers, clerks, police, administrators) and politicians. Since it was government policy to promote the fiction of separate independent nation-states, a corollary was for it to nurture the growth of a middle-class layer to support such independent nation-states.

In 1963, Transkei was the first Native reserve to become a self-governing territory, and in 1976, the first self-governing territory to gain independence as part of the ruling class's Grand Apartheid strategy. K.D. (or, Kaiser Daliwonga) Matanzima – about whom Mda's memoir comments extensively – was its first president.

1994 – The New South Africa

A striking anomaly of the "new" South Africa – a constitutional democracy – is that it has created a space and role for the institution of chieftainship to thrive. Thus, chiefs, who were part of the oppressive machinery of the apartheid state, have seamlessly positioned themselves as a part of the rulership class in the new democratic state.

As long ago as the 1960s, there were commentators who believed that the institution of Chiefs had outlived its usefulness. For example, Govan Mbeki, in his *The Peasant's Revolt*, had the following to say:

> *If Africans have had Chiefs, it was because all human societies have had*
> *them at one stage or another. But when a people have developed to a stage*
> *which discards chieftainship, when their social development contradicts*
> *the need for such an institution, then to force it on them is not liberation*
> *but enslavement. (p. 47)[45]*

---

[44] Ibid.

[45] Quoted in Kepe, T. & Ntsebeza, L. (eds.). 2012. *Rural Resistance in South Africa: The Mpondo Revolts after Fifty Years*. Cape Town: UCT Press.

But perhaps chieftainship is not being forced on the people. Perhaps it's a question of lack of readiness, as suggested by Mafeje,[46] for whom "tribalism" (in this day-and-age) no longer has a material basis – "the material basis of tribes has effectively been destroyed or eroded by the march of history." (p. 258). "But," he critically adds, "the ideology of tribalism persists."

> *Tribalism could be regarded as false consciousness on the part of the supposed tribesmen, who subscribe to an ideology that is inconsistent with their material base and therefore unwittingly respond to the call for their own exploitation. On the part of the new African elite, it is a ploy or distortion they use to conceal their exploitative role. (p. 259)*

In short, tribalism, like racialism, serves ruling class interests by subduing if not stifling, class consciousness, and therefore contributing to the docility of the working class masses.

Commenting on the dual, intermediate role of chiefs in South Africa today, Michael Williams observes that "the ability of chiefs to 'link' the state with society, as well as their ability to act at times autonomously from the state or serve at other times as a functionary of the state, are the chieftaincy's most intriguing features."[47]

Perhaps this should not be surprising when one considers that Chiefs were part of the process that "created" the new South Africa. They were represented at the Codesa negotiating table through their Congress of Traditional Leaders of South Africa (Contralesa), and would certainly have done whatever it took to ensure an outcome favourable to themselves. Laura Phillips points out that "Contralesa was fairly successful in pushing for power in a new democratic South Africa and insisting on the maintenance of customary law and chiefly control over land."[48]

She goes on to show how, post-1994, Contralesa has succeeded in further strengthening the position of Chiefs going forward.

> *The result has been the passing and adoption (and then striking down in 2010) of the Communal Land Rights Act of 2004, the Traditional Leadership and Governance Framework Act, and the Communal Land Tenure Policy. In various ways these laws and policies undermine the*

[46] Mafeje, A. 1971. The Ideology of Tribalism. *The Journal of Modern African Studies*, 9(2):253-261. https://doi.org/10.1017/S0022278X00024927

[47] Williams, J.M. 2004. Leading from behind: democratic consolidation and chieftaincy in South Africa. *Journal of Modern African Studies*, 42(1):113-36. Cambridge University Press. https://doi.org/10.1017/S0022278X03004506

[48] Phillips, L. 2017. History of South Africa's Bantustans. Political History, Social History, Southern Africa. https://doi.org/10.1093/acrefore/9780190277734.013.80

> security of land tenure, give chiefs wide-ranging powers over residents,
> entrench the "tribal boundaries" as set up by the 1951 Tribal Authorities
> Act, and phase out alternative forms of property ownership such as the
> Communal Property Associations. The Traditional Courts Bill is still on the
> table in 2017, threatening to give chiefs sole jurisdiction in presiding over
> "custom," which holds significant consequences for women's land rights in
> the former bantustan regions in which the chiefs are the most powerful.[49]

With Land Reform looming large as the next "big thing" in South Africa there can
be little doubt that Contralesa will be in the thick of things fighting to maintain the
Chiefs' regressive hold on rural society – and in the process, to secure the material
interests of the Chiefs. Again, Laura Phillips's comments are instructive:

> The divvying up of mineral resources in post-apartheid South Africa has
> also been closely linked to the legacy of the bantustans and the growing
> power of the chieftaincy. Under bantustan administration, land was held
> communally by chiefs, with the bantustan state acting as trustee. In the
> mineral-rich bantustans of Bophuthatswana and Lebowa, chiefs often
> leased land to (white-owned) mining companies in exchange for royalties,
> often not fairly distributed to their subjects.

> Furthermore, chiefly authorities and representatives have been welcomed
> into management and administration by mining companies, who in the
> post-1994 period have been trying to fulfill racial quotas and the goals of
> black economic empowerment. The ethnic base to economic success has
> heightened factionalism in royal families and subethnic groups, and ... has
> cleared the way for "unfettered mine expansion through the aegis of these
> new configurations of tribal authority and extractive capital."

The outline and observations in the above paragraphs are meant as a backdrop to the
absorbing narrative-streams so eloquently presented by Mda in his memoir, which
reads by turns like comedy, tragicomedy, drama, melodrama and outright farce. Mda
provides unique close-ups, and in many cases takes us behind the scenes of events of
historical magnitude, revealing again and again the corrupting influence of power.
There is something Shakespearian in the grandiose absurdity that plays out in the
rivalries, connivances, back-biting and betrayals implicit in the many scenarios
depicting the interplay of naked power-struggles; we are apt to agree with Mda when
he says that truth is stranger than fiction. Nowhere is this more evident than in the
at-times-unbelievable depths to which a Kaiser Matanzima would sink to score any

---

49   Ibid.

points off Paramount Sabata Dalindyebo, whom, clearly, he sees as his bitterest rival. And then, more unbelievable: the lavish praise heaped on the arch-apartheid quisling and collaborator Matanzima at his funeral, by South African state president, Thabo Mbeki in 2003.

A moving counterpoint to Matanzima, his masters and other collaborators, are the many victims of their brutality, who remained heroically implacable against the oppressors' onslaughts. At the end of the day, this majestic, inspirational heroism is what the book celebrates.

Mda has a deft pen, and writes with sublime skill and authority. His vantage point gives him unique insight into much of the intimate detail underlying events of sometimes sweeping historical scope, and enables him to provide a deeper factual layer absent from most historical accounts. *Struggle and Hope* reads like a well-crafted thriller, but in no way compromises on historical accuracy. It is a work overlaid by the writer's keen wisdom and genuine caring for the subjects he writes about. There can be little doubt that this "historico-memoir" will come to stand shoulder-to-shoulder with all the other definitive works of its genre.

Centre for the Advancement of Non-Racialism and Democracy (CANRAD)
Nelson Mandela University, Port Elizabeth
January 2019

Chapter 1

Phalo's land

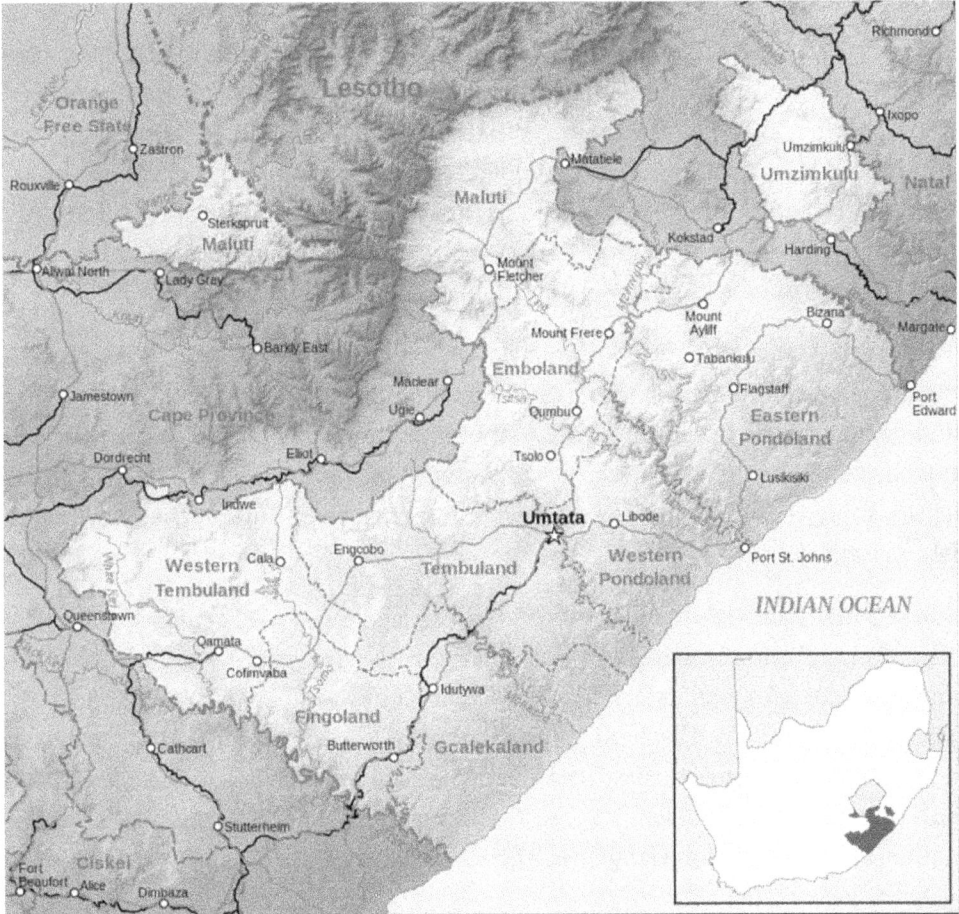

Figure 1.1   Map of Transkei (Wikipedia, November 2018)

Transkei is the name used to refer to that stretch of territory in the south-east of the subcontinent extending from the Great Kei River in the south, to the southern border of the KwaZulu Natal at the Mtamvuna River. It covers all the land east of the Drakensberg Mountain Range down to the Indian Ocean. This is largely choice agricultural land with fertile arable land in abundance, coupled with excellent pasturage that makes it prime land for livestock farming. The biblical reference to Canaan as the "land of milk and honey" comes to mind as a fitting description of the area.

This part of the country is blessed with a moderate climate and handsome annual rainfall. Good rains fall from spring till autumn, but are rather sparse in winter. Before conquest and colonisation, a striking feature of the territory was its verdant pastures and vast herds of cattle and goats. Small wonder the country's inhabitants were proud and successful livestock farmers. Grain production, primarily maize and sorghum, made the territory self-sufficient. The people were prosperous, well nourished, healthy and robust.

The name Transkei is colonial and a misnomer. After all, which side of a river is across and which is not? It has its origin in the fact that the European invaders approached Xhosaland from the south-west (the Western Cape). With their nefarious policy of ethnic cleansing, they uprooted, despoiled and displaced amaXhosa from that vast territory from the Gamtoos River valley right up to the Great Kei River. As previously mentioned, in the process, Xhosaland was wiped off the face of the map and the heart of Xhosaland was renamed, for fine cheek, "British Kaffraria".

The land beyond the Kei was designated as a "Native reserve". Of course, there were other cognate nations in the reserve who had not been involved in the Xhosa's life and death struggle in defence of the fatherland. In many practical ways, they had not been seriously affected by the encroaching invaders. Figuratively, they had been asleep while these momentous events were taking place and on the whole were left unscathed.

The original name of the territory under discussion here is KwaXhosa, meaning Xhosaland. However, within Xhosaland there was territory occupied by the amaMpondo tribe and referred to as "emaMpondweni", that is, "Mpondoland". Similarly, land occupied by the amaXesibe tribe was "emaXesibeni", that was occupied by the amaMpondomise tribe, "emaMpondomiseni", and that was occupied by the amaThembu tribe, "ebaThenjini". All these were components of the bigger Xhosa nation, speaking the same language, Xhosa, and observing Xhosa laws and customs.

The rivers that enrich the territory are the Mzimkhulu, Mzimvubu, Mngazi, Thina, Tsitsa, Mthatha, Mbhashe, Gcuwa and Nciba (the Great Kei River). None of the rivers is navigable. The coast in its pristine splendour became known as "the Wild Coast" with its plethora of rivers and streams that run into the sea, in spectacular wooded gorges.

Under colonial administration, the whole area, 26 districts in all, was governed as a unit under the Chief Magistrate of the Transkeian Territories. Mthatha, the capital of Thembuland, was chosen for its central situation as the capital of the Transkei. The population was African with a sprinkling of Whites in small villages and towns that were growing as administrative centres in every district. From the outset there was no common citizenship or equality between Black and White. The Whites in the territory were the extension of the White government in Cape Town. They were definitely not part of the indigenous populace.

All Whites in the territory occupied land in freehold and their properties were surveyed and they were given title deeds. According to the title deeds, the land was allotted to them by His Britannic Majesty (by the grace of God, King of the United Kingdom of Great Britain, Scotland, Ireland and Wales and the British dominions overseas, Defender of the Faith and Emperor of India).

Surprise of surprises! As amaXhosa, we were brought up under the adage: *God rules in Heaven, but the land is under Phalo*. Not only had these despicable plunderers stolen African land, but they simultaneously obliterated the name of Phalo and substituted it with that of their sovereign who was a super-robber who had stolen other people's lands worldwide. The sheer impudence of imperialists knows no limits!

In their meanness and shamelessness, the White government ensured the disenfranchisement of Africans by the simple ruse of imposing property and educational qualifications in order to qualify for citizenship rights. The towns and villages were run by municipal councils or village management boards elected by the ratepayers. In the case of the Black[50] community, surveys were undertaken in some districts and title deeds were issued in respect of residential sites and arable lots. These were not in freehold, but at the pleasure of the government and could not be sold or pledged as security.

The majority of districts were not surveyed and lot holders were given certificates of occupation. The White government had now arrogated to itself ownership of the land, and issued title deeds and certificates of occupation. All the land occupied by Africans was deemed to be government land and, despite their title deeds or certificates of ownership, the land was regarded as government land on which they resided at government's pleasure. As a result, none of them qualified for the franchise – they were disqualified on the grounds that they were squatters on government land.

After conquest, many Africans saw the need for education and sent their children to school. Education was also the means to get enrolled on the Common Voters' Roll. With the spread of education, there was a steady rise of African numbers on the Voters' Roll. Faced with this alarming and threatening danger of being swamped by African voters, Whites simply abandoned their pretence and dropped all property

---

[50] "Black" is a term that embraces all groups who were regarded as "non-White" or "non-European". These would include "African", "Indian" and "Coloured".

and educational qualifications for Whites and introduced adult franchise. The vote was also extended to White females. In the case of Blacks, the qualifications were made more stringent and were rigidly applied. Registration on the Voters' Roll was not encouraged, but rather made difficult.

After the formation of the Union of South Africa in 1910, Transkei was demarcated as the Thembuland constituency. Of course, the correct and sensible name was Xhosaland, but the name Xhosa was anathema and Thembu had softer and more pleasant connotations. Further proof that Africans were quick on the uptake was provided when Dr W.B. Rubusana was elected as Member of the Provincial Council (MPC) for Thembuland. Unfortunately, this was to be not only the first, but also the last time an African was so elected. During his tenure, he and Dr Abdurahman, who was classified "Coloured", were the only Black faces in the all-White Cape Provincial Council. During the election, a doubting White voter had asked Dr Rubusana what assurance he would give that Whites could entrust their fate to him. He replied assuringly, "I am for all the people of this constituency, but of course the proof of the pudding is in the eating thereof".

Dr Rubusana's tenure as MPC was short and ended in a cloud of tribal acrimony. He had not failed as representative, but in fact, had been capable, diligent, astute and articulative. When new elections came, he stood for re-election, but unfortunately Mr John Tengo Jabavu also came forward as a candidate. Both were eminent leaders in the African community and in the heat of campaigning, the African vote split along tribal lines. AmaXhosa voted for Rubusana, a Xhosa man of the Cirha clan, while the amaMfengu voted for Jabavu, a Mfengu man of the Jili clan. Both of them lost and A.O.B. Payn, the White candidate, profited from the split and won with the solid support of the White vote.

The contest between these African stalwarts was to have a devastating effect on the African community and was to bedevil Xhosa-Mfengu relations for years. Later a story emerged that this had all been a White plot and that Jabavu had taken the bait unwittingly. The campaign was dirty and bitter and fueled strong feelings that, as in former years during the wars of dispossession, amaMfengu were ever-ready to be used by Whites against amaXhosa. Although the campaign degenerated into a bitter Xhosa-Mfengu feud, it would be erroneous to suggest that all Jabavu supporters were actuated by an anti-Xhosa sentiment.

There were those who genuinely believed that Jabavu was the better candidate on merit. One should keep in mind that Dr Rubusana was an ordained minister and there were voters who were not happy with a minister abandoning his congregation and entering the political arena.

On reflection, however, it is difficult not to blame Jabavu for being selfish, short-sighted and narrow-minded. Surely, he should have foreseen the acrimony that was the outcome of his attempt to oust Dr Rubusana, so why did he do it? What is more, he must have realised that a split in the African vote would open the door for the White candidate. African nationalism was still in the making and "Fingo People" were still tightly held by the British imperialist apron strings.

Chapter 2

Conquest, colonisation and oppression

Of all the Xhosa-speaking people, abaThembu are second to none in their strict adherence to and observance of Xhosa customs, traditions, language and usage. One may say this is rather strange when taking cognisance of the fact that by all accounts, abaThembu, have a different lineage from amaXhosa.

AmaXhosa claim descent from Xhosa,[51] whereas abaThembu trace their ancestry to Zwide and the two lines are completely distinct. For all that, what seems to matter most is that, through their long historical association, close proximity and intercourse, a strong affinity was engendered and cultivated. Whatever differences might have existed initially have dissolved and been almost completely eliminated. It is further evident that the stronger influence came from amaXhosa and it was amaXhosa who set the common standard and moulded the character and norms of both groups. Still, abaThembu were not absorbed and retained their identity and nationhood.

It appears the only notable contribution by abaThembu was the institution of polygamy which unto this day is still called the Thembu system ("isithembu"). AbaThembu even adopted the Xhosa (ingqithi), the characteristic lopping off of the tip of the small finger on the left hand. The relations between amaXhosa and abaThembu have always been warm and each royal house has valued taking a bride from the other. It almost became a question of first choice. In consequence, amaXhosa and abaThembu became closely related. It is generally agreed that it is the amaXhosa who led the migration southward from Central Africa, but the amaMpondomise and abaThembu were not far behind. AmaXhosa finally ensconced themselves and established their kingdom and predominance in the south-east of the sub-continent. Along the coast, the land was inhabited by amaXhosa with abaThembu on their right flank in the interior, the two living side by side, in peace and concord.

---

[51] According to SA History Online: "Stories and legends provide accounts of Xhosa ancestral heroes. According to one oral tradition, the first person on Earth was a great leader called Xhosa. Another tradition stresses the essential unity of the Xhosa-speaking people by proclaiming that all the Xhosa subgroups are descendants of one ancestor, Tshawe. Historians have suggested that Xhosa and Tshawe were probably the first Xhosa kings or paramount (supreme) chiefs." Online: https://www.sahistory.org.za/article/xhosa [Accessed 19 November 2018].

In their northward push from the Cape Peninsula, the European invaders and would-be colonisers came up against amaXhosa in the Gamtoos River valley. AmaXhosa were able to contain and even push back the encroaching Boers, but the arrival of the British altered the equation. While the military power of amaXhosa was able to thwart the tempo and the momentum of the British intrusion and invasion, the superior arms and organisation of the predators prevailed and amaXhosa were defeated and displaced. It was amaXhosa who bore the brunt of the land grabbing and dispossession. On the whole, abaThembu were not directly affected until much later, when during the Eighth War of Dispossession [1851-1853] hostilities spilled over to the adjacent abaThembu. The latter did not show the hardiness and doggedness of their Xhosa compatriots. For the first time, Thembu land was overrun and abaThembu displaced by the usual British policy of ethnic cleansing. AbaThembu lost the Lukhanji region where their royal place was situated (the Queenstown district and its environs).

The colonisers always expropriated the natives from the choicest land. Such land was said to be favourable and suitable for European occupation. Again, when the crafty and sinister plotter, the Cape Governor, Sir George Grey, was taking mean advantage of the famished and weakened amaXhosa after the Nongqawuse calamity and uprooting them from their ancestral land, abaThembu also did not escape unscathed. They were driven out of their territory and forced onto the land in the upper Kei region from which the amaGcaleka/amaXhosa had been evicted. The relocated abaThembu were then called "emigrant abaThembu".

By this time, the Thembu monarch Mtirara had died and it was his mother, the dowager, Queen Nonesi, who was at the receiving end of the British colonial expansion. The Regent Joyi was far away in Mthatha in the north-east corner of Thembuland. The British forced Nonesi to the Glen Grey area before expelling her and forcing her to return to her maiden home in Mpondoland (emaMpondweni). Mtirara's son, the young heir Ngangelizwe, was brought to Mthatha by the Regent Joyi. Mtirara's son of the Right-Hand House, Matanzima, was in the group of abaThembu who were made "emigrant abaThembu" and settled on the territory taken from amaXhosa. Mtirara's son Mfanta, of a junior house, went to settle at Mbinzana in the Glen Grey district.

Great House
NGUBENGCUKA

Right Hand House
JUMBA   MDUKISWA   **MGUDLWA**

Great House
MTIRARA   JOYI   Right Hand House MNQANQENI   Left Hand House MANDELA   FALO

Great House **NGANGELIZWE**   Right Hand House **MATANZIMA**   Left Hand House MFANTA   Great House GOBINAMBA   Right Hand House MAKAULA   QAQAWULI

DALINDYEBO   SILIMELA   NDUMISO   MVUZO   MGUBHULI   **ZWELIBHANGILE**   ZANEGQELE   GADLA   KHAWULELE

JONGINTABA   SAMPU (Jongilizwe)   DABULAMANZI   BUSOBENGWE   MHLOBO   MARHELANE (Bangilizwe)   DALAGUBHA   THWALIMFENE   DUMISANI

JUSTICE (Zwelivumile)   SABATA   BAMBILANGA   MATOTI   NONKENYANA   ZWELIHLE   KAISER DALIWONGA   GEORGE   ROLIHLAHLA

BUYELEKHAYA   ZONDWA   NDABA

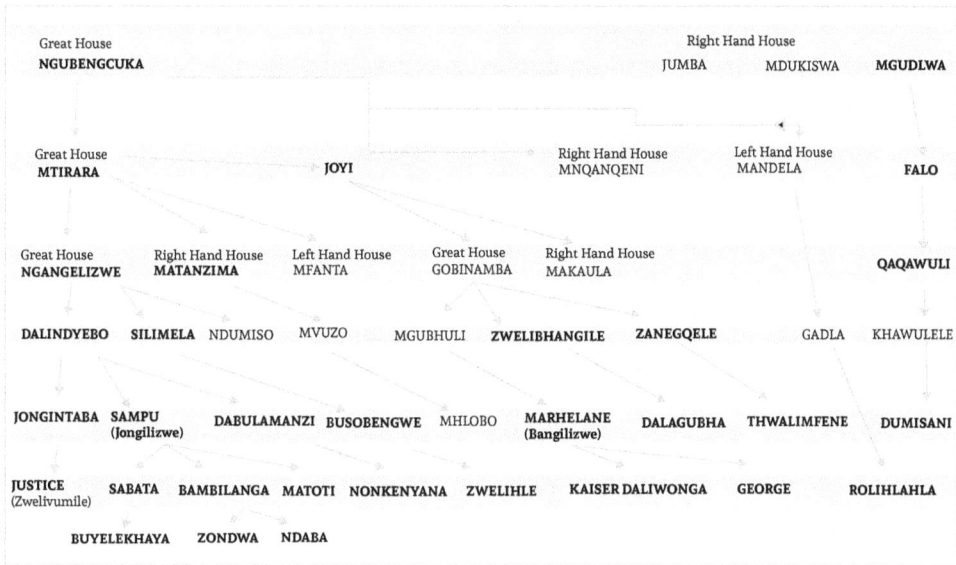

Figure 1.2   Abathembu Genealogy – Compiled by the author Mda Mda, 2019.

In due course, Ngangelizwe took over the reigns as Thembu sovereign. The district of Glen Grey had by then been excised from Thembuland and become part of the Cape Colony. Of course, the inhabitants were abaThembu and Glen Grey was the first "Native Reserve" under colonial rule. When Thembuland was annexed to the Cape Colony many years later, Glen Grey remained outside Thembuland although it was and still is Thembu territory and inhabited by abaThembu.

Ngangelizwe had an ungovernable temper and was a sadistic brute. During one of his bouts of uncontrollable rage in 1873, he savagely assaulted his wife, Queen Novili, daughter of the Xhosa King Sarhili. The queen's younger sister, Nongxokozelo, was staying with her sister at the Thembu Great Place and was present during the assault. The gruesome spectacle was too much for her and she tried to intervene by coming between the two.

For her impudence in daring to come between His Majesty and his victim/wife, Ngangelizwe turned his wrath on her and beat her to a pulp. The Xhosa royal house was aghast at this shocking news. What made matters worse was that Ngangelizwe was unremorseful. He was unapologetic and totally unconcerned as if nothing had happened. After the contemptuous and off-hand manner in which Sir George Grey had treated the Xhosa King Sarhili in the aftermath of the Nongqawuse national catastrophe, Ngangelizwe believed amaXhosa were a spent force and he had nothing to fear from them.

However, amaXhosa could not ignore this outrage and affront and the king dispatched a punitive force to teach this brute some manners. When the Gcaleka Impi came down the Mbhashe Valley heading for Thembuland, consternation seized the Thembu villagers near the border. The crossing point was the ford leading to Mthentu on the Thembu side. Mthentu was inhabited by the amaZizi tribe under Chief Menziwa, who had been asked, when applying for land, whether they were man enough to stand up to an invading force. They had promised to do their duty "like men" if the need arose.

It is said that amaZizi of Menziwa were as good as their word and made a determined stand against amaGcaleka. However, they finally gave way as they were up against redoubtable fighters. The story goes that the Mthentu men offered the only resistance the Gcaleka force encountered. For the rest, abaThembu ran for dear life. The Thembu monarch, Ngangelizwe himself, did not do any better and did not set a good example. It is said that the corpulent monarch nearly choked as he fled to Clarkebury Mission in Engcobo district. There he dashed into Reverend Peter Hargreaves's house and sneaked into the bedroom where he cowered under a bed, visibly shaken.

The British colonialists, who were always plotting and engaging in intrigue, saw their chance. The Cape Governor sent word to Ngangelizwe advising that the only security from Gcaleka fury was British protection. Ngangelizwe gladly accepted British protection and Thembuland was accordingly annexed by the Cape Colony. With annexation, Thembuland came under the direct rule and administration of the colonial government in Cape Town. With the formation of the Transkeian territories, Thembuland fell under the Chief Magistrate of the Transkeian Territories, Major Sir Henry Elliot.

It was Ngangelizwe himself who surrendered the independence of the Thembu nation. He now became a mere figurehead and received a modest stipend from the government. In 1877, the ninth and last War of Dispossession broke out. The Xhosa King, Sarhili, found himself under unprovoked attack by the colonial forces. True to form, the Cape Governor called upon the Thembu to support the colonial forces and Ngangelizwe agreed. They were used mostly along the Mbhashe River. For his help to the colony, Ngangelizwe was given the district of Elliotdale which was taken from amaGcaleka. Thembuland under Ngangelizwe consisted of the six districts, Mthatha, Ngcobo, St Mark's, Xhalanga, Mqanduli and Elliotdale. The Thembu sovereign was regarded as a trustworthy and dependable supporter of the colonial government. AbaThembu, like amaMfengu, were considered to be "good and loyal natives". Ngangelizwe's faults and failings were overlooked. According to the British way of justice, political correctness was the supreme virtue.

Ngangelizwe's son and heir, Dalindyebo, had taken over rule of the Thembu after his father's death. Unlike his temperamental father, Dalindyebo had a genial nature and friendly disposition. Because he was kind and soft spoken with a dignified bearing, people felt at ease in his presence.

The Union of South Africa was formed in 1910 and the First World War broke out in 1914, but there is nothing noteworthy on record regarding abaThembu, except the good relations forged between Dalindyebo's father and the colonial government which continued undisturbed under the South African government and his placid reign.

Major Sir Henry Elliot had a benevolent tenure as Chief Magistrate of the Transkeian territories. He was popularly known as "Meje" and continued as Chief Magistrate until the early 20th century. After their defeat during the Ninth (and last) War of Dispossession [1877-1878]), amaXhosa looked askance at the colonial government and administration and thus kept their contact to the barest minimum. Even when local structures like the Bhunga Advisory Council were introduced, they showed no inclination to participate.

Major Sir Henry Elliot took it upon himself to approach and try to persuade important members of the royal house, such as Chief Lindinxiwa, younger brother to the Xhosa monarch, Sarhili, who had fled. He spoke to Chief Lindinxiwa, as well as Chief Sigidi of the Mbede in Idutywa and Chief Mcothama of Centane, imploring them to not remain aloof, but to participate in the new dispensation.

They listened respectfully and asked some probing questions. Realising they were being asked to come forward and serve the conqueror, they said they had heard. However, they were not charmed. When Sir Henry Elliot finally retired, the Thembu monarch, Dalindyebo, in a magnificent gesture and show of gratitude for the warm relations between the Thembu royal house and the Chief Magistrate gave him, as a parting gift, a hundred head of cattle. Because the Major was regarded as a man of peace, all the cattle were polled to emphasise the point. Major Elliot accepted the gift, but had the cattle sold and the proceeds donated to a fund he launched for the building of a hospital in Mthatha. When the hospital was built, it was named Sir Henry Elliot Hospital in honour of the Chief Magistrate who wanted to leave something of real value to the people of the Transkei.

Chapter 3

AbaThembu – A house divided

Dalindyebo was middle-aged when he died in 1920. He was succeeded by his son and heir, the short-tempered Sampu, whose royal name was Jongilizwe.

Sampu was the son of Dalindyebo and the Bhaca princess who became Queen Nohajisi. According to custom, Nohajisi was the one who would bear the heir. Her dowry was accordingly paid by Thembu people.

At the time, the South African government was headed by General J.B.M. Hertzog of the NP. The rigid colour bar and entrenchment of white supremacy were the hallmarks of their Nationalist policy. The strident tone of the government and its officials made the African community worried and restive and there was fear that Sampu would not tolerate the abrasive Nationalist stance. However, Sampu did not live long and died prematurely in 1928 after a short illness. His son and heir, Sabata, was born in the same year.

Jongintaba David, who was chief at Mqekezweni, was one of Sampu's half-brothers. He was the eldest of Dalindyebo's sons and was chosen as regent for the young heir, Sabata. As regent, Jongintaba ruled from Mqekezweni. He was a fine figure of a man, dark and handsome. His outlook was progressive and he encouraged and supported education and enlightenment. He understood his responsibilities and took his duties seriously, and discharged them with dignity and finesse. The Thembu people were happy and contented.

The modest stipend the regent received was not enough for his family's needs and could not be stretched to cover the needs of dowager Novoti and her family. As a result, Novoti and Sampu's other two widows were cash strapped. Even the Bumbane royal home became neglected and gradually looked run down and dilapidated. It can therefore never be said that the young Sabata ever lived in opulence. Sampu's widows struggled. They lived and looked like ordinary Thembu folk. Perhaps this was a blessing in disguise for the young Sabata to grow up as an ordinary Thembu boy. His oneness with the Thembu and his dedication to their welfare was the dominant trait in his character and outlook.

The son of Mtirara in the Right-Hand House was Matanzima who, with three other chiefs – Ndarala of the Ndungwana, Gecelo of the Gcina and Stokwe of the Tshatshu – were settled on the land from which the Xhosa were evicted by Sir George Grey. Matanzima's Great Place was at Qamata, in the Cofimvaba district. His eldest son and heir was Mvuzo, whose son was Mhlobo, the father of Kaiser Daliwonga.[52] Chief Mhlobo and the uneducated Qamata residents admired the progressive and educated Mgudlwas of Qhumanco. The Mgudlwas were of the senior Right-Hand House of abaThembu, the Jumba House and Chief Falo Mgudlwa was an ardent proponent of education and change and introduced schools in his territory.

Chief Mhlobo chose Chief Mpondombini Mgudlwa who had been educated at Lovedale, as the custodian of his son, Kaiser Daliwonga. Chief Mpondombini's eldest son, Hulley Oyama, was already at Lovedale when Kaiser went to live at Qhumanco. Kaiser was to follow Hulley and go to Lovedale where he passed his Standard 6 in 1931. Kaiser was a bright and promising student, always up there with the best. He was deservedly awarded a scholarship by the United Transkeian Territories General Council. Hulley had proceeded from Lovedale to Fort Hare, University but did not finish his studies, as he had to make way for his siblings who were also coming to high school.

Kaiser then enrolled at Lovedale High School where he passed the Junior Certificate and Matric before crossing over to Fort Hare for his BA degree. He completed this in 1939. It was Kaiser Daliwonga's honour to be the first from all the Xhosa-speaking royal houses to obtain a degree. It is said that Kaiser acquired his taste for fine clothes, neatness and decorum from the Mgudlwa home. Unlike the Mgudlwas, to whom it appeared natural, with him it looked borrowed and put on and he looked stiff and self-conscious, not relaxed and at ease. He was always composed, had a dignified bearing and was not given to flippant talk. At Lovedale, Kaiser got no favoured treatment and was treated the same as the other students. The only members of a royal house who received preferential treatment were Seretse Khama from the Bamangwato in Bechuanaland (today's Botswana) and those of the Moshesh family from Basutoland (Lesotho). Their Xhosa contemporaries enjoyed no such preferential treatment. It appeared as if the British bore a grudge against amaXhosa. For instance, Gladstone Magqagana Maqoma (Regent Maqoma's grandson) was treated as just another "native boy" when in fact he should have been the pride of Lovedale, not only being a Xhosa prince, but a local one. Lovedale was built on choice land taken from Maqoma when he was regent during the 1834-1835 war. Perhaps one should

---

52   In the text, the author refers to Kaiser Matanzima either as "Kaiser" or "Kaiser Daliwonga" or "K.D." interchangeably.

not have been surprised at the way Gladstone was treated, as Maqoma's grandson Ndabemfene was living at Ntselamanzi, next door to Lovedale, but was treated as a commoner and not the royalty he was.

Kaiser's graduation in autumn 1940 was a big occasion not only for him, but for all the Thembu people. As expected, Kaiser did not seek employment, but went back to Qamata to serve as chief. The miserable pittance he drew from the government was indeed peanuts. He implored the government to pay him like other graduates, for instance teachers, who received the sum of 15 pounds (R30,00) per month.

The government was not impressed and replied curtly that educational qualifications were not taken into account when determining the remuneration of chiefs. For good measure, the government added that he was just one of the many petty chiefs in the Thembuland and, even in his own district, there were other chiefs of equal rank and only three administrative areas looked up to him as chief. Not one to give up easily, Kaiser did not just sit at Qamata and mope. He handed over the reins of chieftainship to his uncle, Dalubuhle, and joined the firm of Hemming & Hughes in Mthatha to do articles of clerkship so as to qualify as an attorney.

On completing his legal training, Kaiser again approached the government, but this time he asked for jurisdiction to enable him to hear and try cases in his court in Qamata. Again his request fell on deaf ears. This time, the government told him only the Thembu monarch had the jurisdiction and he should approach the regent Dabulamanzi, who had taken over after the death of Jongintaba, for his approval. Because the government was not keen to assist him, it sabotaged his plans. The regent visited Mthatha on some other business and the Chief Magistrate asked him if Kaiser had made his request to him.

The regent replied in the negative. The Magistrate then commented tellingly, "These educated ones evidently look down upon and despise their uneducated seniors. Kaiser was here asking for jurisdiction over Qamata and we told him he should get your approval. We will hear from you and not him."

When Kaiser later appeared at the Thembu Great Place, the atmosphere had already been poisoned and the court was prejudiced against him. He was asked testingly why he brought his request to the Great Place. He replied innocently, "I am your child and this is my home. I am aware it is proper for me to come to you with my request. As my fathers, you will present my case to the White government."

Kaiser had spoken respectfully and eloquently and ordinarily the court would have given him a warm welcome and readily acceded to his request. However, because the Chief Magistrate had already planted suspicion in their minds, a spokesperson for the regent addressed him mockingly, saying, "When you went to the Chief Magistrate with your request behind our backs, had you forgotten who your fathers are? Or do you take us cheaply as ignorant uneducated reds (amaQaba)[53] while you are smart and educated?"

In short, the assistance sought was not forthcoming and Kaiser went away empty-handed and dejected.

The author's father, Simeon Slingsby Mda, was interpreter/clerk at the Chief Magistrate's Office. Like many others, he wished Kaiser well and was disappointed when he learnt that Kaiser had been rebuffed at the Great Place. He pleaded with Dabulamanzi and his Councillors to forgive Kaiser's bungling and grant him the jurisdiction he sought. He argued that in fact and by custom, every chief had jurisdiction over his area and it was colonial policy that emasculated chiefs and deprived them of their powers. He also asked them how many cases had come from St Mark's (Kaiser's home district) in the past year. They told him that only three had come. He then said that St Mark's was far from the Great Place and people found it convenient to use the Cofimvaba Magistrate's Court and the services of Mr John Henderson Walker, the attorney there.

They were adamant and would not relent, complaining, "Why did he not come clean and reveal his mistake?" So, Kaiser went back to Qamata with his Attorney's Admission Certificate, but was still denied jurisdiction in his court. In the meantime, his younger brother George Mzimvubu, a BSc graduate from Fort Hare, left teaching and served articles of clerkship with attorney Qunta of Engcobo. On completion, he opened his own offices and practised at Engcobo as a successful attorney.

The Regent Jongintaba was middle-aged when he passed away in 1942. The heir, Sabata, was still in his teens and still at primary school. The senior in the Thembu royal house was Chief Melithafa of Sithebe in Mthatha, but he was already in failing health and declined to take up the regency following Jongintaba's death. Thus, it fell to Chief Dabulamanzi of the Right-Hand House, to take on the onerous, but thankless task. He was chief at Xhongorha in the Mthatha district. Unlike most royalty, he was a simple, unambitious and unpretentious soul.

If looks and physical build were what maketh a man, then Dabulamanzi was an excellent specimen. Tall, dark and handsome, with a smooth complexion, he stood out in any crowd. He was not only a fine man to look at, but was easy going and unsuspecting. He was not astute or on guard and not a match for the wiles and guile of

---

[53]   A derogatory term for uneducated people.

the ever-scheming White government officials. What made him most vulnerable was that he did not seem to grasp the great responsibility and decision-making attached to the regency. He was a loner with no followers with him or in his court. As Thembu observers wryly commented, he was more a tame ox than bull of the herd.

The Second World War was a trying time and people were becoming restive and worried. The government of Field Marshal Smuts was buying time and trying to appease a growing discontented public by using the war as an excuse, and promising an end of their troubles when the war was over. When the war ended, people expected real change and an end to their suffering. However, even before the war was over, the government was already up to its dirty tricks. It launched the nefarious Rehabilitation Scheme in 1945. What incensed people most was the declared intention of the government measures, viz. to reduce the numbers of livestock. The government took the view that the reserves were already over-populated. In consequence, pasturage and grazing land had decreased, but people still imagined they could raise as much livestock as their forebears did. The resultant overstocking and overgrazing led to rapid deterioration of the land, soil erosion and poor grazing. The livestock was now poor and getting poorer and had to be reduced to the determined carrying capacity of the land. The cardinal feature of the rehabilitation scheme was thus stock limitation.

The argument in favour of stock limitation was plausible if the land mass were to remain fixed, but the people – the peasantry in particular – were not impressed. They said the Europeans had colossal cheek after taking people's land for European farms and now accusing them of being too many and carrying too much livestock on too little land. The South African Parliament passed the Act and, as it was during the 1945 session of the Bhunga (the United Transkeian Territories General Council), the matter was presented to the Bhunga for its acceptance.

What the Bhunga usually did when faced with a contentious issue, was to ask that the matter be referred to the districts to test public opinion. It was always the easy way out of a tight corner and a means to defeat an unpopular measure. However, somehow this ruse did not work this time and the Bhunga members were outwitted by the magistrates and the Bhunga surprisingly tamely accepted this measure.

The outcry from every corner of the Transkei was loud and ominous. People were likening the scheme to a declaration of war against the people. They threatened that the government would get what it had asked for. The Bhunga members, usually respected leaders and representatives in their communities, were condemned and disowned as stooges of the government.

Because of the strong and openly-expressed opposition to the measures, the government wisely announced that it would not be proceeding with enforcement of the scheme in spite of the Bhunga's acceptance. The government hoped to avert this threatening civil war the rehabilitation scheme was likely to provoke.

However, the government was not abandoning the scheme outright. Instead, each magistrate was enjoined to visit every administrative area in his district in an all-out campaign to convince and cajole residents to accept the system. The magistrates were to make it as attractive as possible. If people agreed, then and only then would the government proclaim the area a betterment area and amenities would be provided to make the scheme attractive.

The Mthatha magistrate spoke to the well-disposed, but unsuspecting regent (Dabulamanzi) intimating that the government wished to bring to the attention of Transkei residents the urgent need and great benefits of the rehabilitation scheme. In pursuance of that objective, he had drawn up an itinerary to visit all administrative areas in the district. Because he did not wish to go behind the regent's back, he wanted the regent to be present at every meeting. He said that that would ensure the regent would be able to monitor and keep under scrutiny his talks with abaThembu. This invitation appeared well meant and innocent and the regent readily agreed to accompany the magistrate.

As it turned out, the Thembu masses did not find the exercise innocent. In fact, they found it crooked and insidious. At the very first meeting at Sithebe, local residents took exception at the unexpected attendance of the regent as a member of the magistrate's entourage. After the magistrate had made his eloquent and persuasive address, he invited questions or comments from the audience. The tone and mood of the residents was set by the very first speaker from the floor. He put their distress politely, saying, "We are bamboozled and dumbfounded and unable to speak. You rightly tell us you are our visitor, but we are gravely handicapped and in fact tongue-tied. According to custom and tradition, the regent is our head and father and he should have been with us and one of us to welcome you. Now he has come with you, in your party. Who now among us is in a position to welcome you? What can we say and on whose behalf?"

That should have been a wake-up call for the regent to server ties with the magistrate and his party and be with the people. It is said, none are as blind as those who will not see, nor any as deaf as those who refuse to listen. Instead of divorcing himself from the magistrate and leaving him to his devices, the regent continued on the magistrate's itinerary. He thought it would suffice if at the beginning of each meeting he announced disarmingly, "I am not here to influence you one way or the other. I am not taking any side in the matter. I want you to feel free and to make your choice or decision on this issue without fear." On hearing these words, one peasant said sadly, "Do you hear him? He says he is taking no side and therefore is not on our side. Is he no longer our regent?"

Regent Dabulamanzi wanted the impossible. He could not be neutral on crucial matters and still be head of the Thembu nation. He was required to endorse an action and give effect to the majority view and make it the official view. As he continued with the magistrate's itinerary, people grew exasperated and rebellious. Some even rebuked him openly, asking, "What are you doing in the government's party? Why do you allow yourself to be dragged around the country? Have you forgotten you are head of the Thembu nation?"

The magistrate reaped no benefits from the itinerary, but for the regent, the exercise was a complete disaster. People grew to despise him and opposition to him mounted until some openly hated him. Poor Dabulamanzi refused to learn the ABCs of winning the people's hearts and minds, viz. to be with the people and on their side unreservedly. He learned nothing from the itinerary bungle, believing his good intentions were misunderstood or that some evil-minded people twisted the facts and deceived the masses. Unfortunately for him, this was not the last hurdle he would struggle against. There were yet more to come.

Before the regent had had time to recover from the public relations disaster of the rehabilitation scheme episode, he was again required to show his mettle. This time it was in the full glare of the elite of the Transkei and the Transkei public at large. The occasion was the much publicised royal visit by the British sovereign King George VI, the queen and the two princesses to South Africa in 1947. As usual, such occasions are characterised by an organised display of pomp and power to impress the masses, the "vulgus", as the Romans would say.

Chapter 4

Sabata ascends throne

The visit to the Transkei, the biggest native reserve, was the highlight and showpiece of the royal visit. The tribal leaders, their followers and the population at large would be invited to Mthatha to meet the royal guests. In preparation for the great day, the Thembu regent, the Mpondo sovereign and the Xhosa monarch were invited to Mthatha to sign the speech to be read and presented to King George VI on behalf of the people of Transkei. Embossed in gold letters, the scroll would be taken to the British Isles as a memento.

The speech had been prepared and written by the White government officials who knew best what speech would fittingly be made on the Natives' behalf. Of course, the Natives could not be trusted to be capable of preparing such a speech themselves. The chosen venue for the august occasion was on the outskirts of Mthatha in the present Fort Gale area above the Mthatha/Engcobo road. It was a fine autumn day in 1947 as hundreds descended upon Mthatha from all sides dressed in their finery. Gone were the days of yore when skin karosses, leather skirts made from cowhide and ornaments of beads were the rage. This was now the mid-20th century and almost all wore modern dress.

All were in a festive mood and eager to see for themselves the mighty British monarch on whose worldwide empire the sun never sets. The protocol devised by White officialdom was that, as Mthatha is on the border of Thembuland and Mpondoland, both the Thembu Paramount Dabulamanzi and the Mpondo Paramount Botha Sigcau[54] would go together to present the scroll to the British monarch. The story goes that, at the appropriate time, both stood up and proceeded to the dais on which his Britannic Majesty sat. The precious gift, the scroll, was in the hands of Dabulamanzi as they moved up. The two made an imposing sight as they moved majestically forward.

Both Dabulamanzi and Botha were tall, dark-complexioned and clean-shaven. It was Dabulamanzi who had the better looks and physique, as Botha looked rather overweight. When they reached the dais as per instructions, Dabulamanzi gave the scroll to Botha and it was Botha who handed it to King George VI. In consternation

---

[54] Also referred to as Botha Sigcawu.

and disbelief, the Thembu who were sitting in front and saw this happen exclaimed audibly. "What is this stupid bungler doing? Now the British monarch will believe the Thembu are the vassals of the Mpondo! Is this fellow mad?"

That is how the day was spoilt for abaThembu and in their own territory. Suddenly, it became a day of shame! Of course, amaMpondo were gloating. Everything had gone their way. They were the cock of the walk. They were champions of the Transkei and Mthatha was theirs. Keen observers were to say abaThembu were never in the picture at all and it had been amaMpondo's day from the beginning. If numbers were counted, surely abaThembu outnumbered amaMpondo by far, but the Thembu thousands counted for nothing. It was amaMpondo who were in the limelight and they had stolen the show early in the day. When it came to staging a fine show or a spectacle you could bet on amaMpondo and they knew how to seize a good opportunity.

In this case, the amaMpondo had arranged to assemble at a point, "Faku's Stone", beyond Ncambedlana on the outskirts of Mthatha. From as far afield as Mbizana on the coast and other places in East Mpondoland, Mpondo men had come to Mthatha on horseback. Those from West Mpondoland awaited their brethren from the east at the agreed spot. The amaMpondo had arranged with the Mthatha municipality that the Mpondo procession would start crossing the Mthatha Bridge at 9 a.m. on the day of the royal visit. Forget the fiction that there is something called "African time". At 9 a.m. sharp, the head of the Mpondo column entered the Mthatha Bridge.

People who witnessed the cavalcade say it was an unforgettable sight as thousands of horsemen descended from Ncambedlana down Hillcrest, past Norwood, four deep, in military formation. At the head of the column were the Mpondo royalty surrounding Botha, their sovereign. Praise singers had a field day as amaMpondo showed off as they entered Mthatha in formation. As the Mthatha traffic officers guided the convoy up York Road, then onto Sutherland Street and westwards towards Fort Gale, the rear column was still winding up the east corner of Ncambedlana, the present day South Africa National Tuberculosis Association (SANTA) Hospital.

The story goes that the dowager, Thembu Queen Novoti, was on her way to Fort Gale and still at the corner of Owen Street and Sutherland Street when the Mpondo column appeared. As the buoyant Mpondo horsemen rode past, someone in her group remarked teasingly, "You say this is Thembuland! Can't you see amaMpondo have taken over and are riding high in your capital?" Novoti was moved to tears and that was still in the morning long before the Dabulamanzi gaffe during the climax of the ceremony. AbaThembu were an amorphous mass and their leaders lacked imagination.

The regency's reign at the time had been long for the simple reason that the heir, Sabata, was an infant when his father, Sampu Jongilizwe, died. Jongintaba had been at the helm as regent for 13 years. After him, Dabulamanzi had been holding the reins for a mere five years, but to the disgruntled Thembu, it was as if it had been an eternity. The question on everyone's lips was, "When will this nightmare end?" Fortunately, there were good reasons for giving the ready and comforting answer, "sooner rather than later".

The heir was in his late teens, in the pink of condition and pulsating with youthful vigour. The Thembu way to manhood is by circumcision, not by reaching 21 years, the European so-called age of adulthood. Sabata was now 18 years of age, but at school, still in Standard 8, and actually lagging behind his age group. It had been hoped that he would complete Matric at least. Kaiser Matanzima had set a high benchmark with a BA degree, plus a legal qualification. To the majority, however, education was desirable, but not a *sine qua non*. In fact, natural intelligence was rated higher than a good education.

It was not Sabata's family, nor the house of Mtirara, the Thembu royal house, who brought matters to a head. The ordinary tribesmen, the so-called commoners, mounted a vigorous propaganda campaign urging that the heir should go for circumcision. This popular clamour and public sentiment forced the hand of the royal house. Yielding to the popular demand and pressure, Sabata went for circumcision before he had reached 20 years, as was the custom. In his case, the popular adage "circumstances alter cases" applied. He was a special case.

To go for circumcision does not signal that one is terminating one's schooling. In Sabata's case, no one imagined that he would be taken out of school. When schools reopened and it was time for him to return to school, he was still busy attending presentation functions. Invitations were coming thick and fast and the young man was being paraded around the country. Sabata himself was enjoying his first public exposure while many ordinary Thembu folk were having this first glimpse of and personal contact with the charming young man.

He was handsome with a broad, attractive face, but more importantly, he was pleasant to talk to, intelligent and articulate. Eager to show off the heir, a particular group had him attend the quarterly meeting the magistrate held with the chiefs, headmen and their followers. Hoping to create a fine impression, they introduced the smart young man to the magistrate in his chambers. The magistrate received them politely, but the interview was short. At the quarterly meeting, the magistrate referred to the interview and congratulated the heir on reaching manhood, adding that the young man had all the good signs of a promising future. He said he hoped the young man would complete his studies.

Warming up to his subject, the magistrate observed that there was no threat to his position and it was important for him to prepare and equip himself to be able to fill the position competently. He stressed the importance of a good education, particularly in the modern age. He added that there was a time for everything and youth was the time to learn. He said he hoped abaThembu would not be short-sighted and cut short the young man's education. Because his position was secure, he urged abaThembu to make sure he returned to school without delay. He ended by saying he wished him and the Thembu nation well.

I want to believe that in expressing these sentiments, the magistrate, J.J. Yates, had no ulterior motive and, in fact. thought he was promoting the best interests and welfare of the heir. Unluckily, it can be stated for the record that his motives were misconstrued and his well-meant advice not well-received. The majority of Thembu peasants had come to regard the regent as a drawback. They were clamouring for a change and what better change than for the prince to take over? In their mood, they gained the impression that the magistrate wished to postpone Sabata's succession for as long as possible and *pari passu*, to extend (for the government) the favourable regency, for as long as possible.

Try as hard as they could, they could not hide their chagrin and disappointment. For one thing, the government gave no assistance, monetary or otherwise, towards the education of the children of chiefs. In Sabata's case, the government heretofore had not shown any interest in his education and was now giving unsolicited advice. AbaThembu knew what they wanted, and this was a pure Thembu affair that did not call for any government meddling. In this charged atmosphere, those abaThembu who held a contrary view – and there were many – decided it was best to keep their views to themselves. Inevitably, the young Sabata found the views of those who favoured his take-over more persuasive. As a result, he did not return to school.

While it is true that a sound education provides a good foundation for a knowledgeable and well-balanced human being, at the time, most chiefs had not even had the benefit of a secondary education, which Sabata had. With his secondary school education, he was one of the better educated. In fact, his outlook and deportment evinced both good breeding and enlightenment. He was always a man of impeccable manners and civility and showed a maturity far beyond his years.

On the question of his return to school, most Thembu spokesmen felt that the question had been overtaken by events. What is more, they were convinced that he was ready to carry the heavy burden of kingship. They brought matters to a head by confronting the regent on the issue. The regent had never been a difficult person. On the contrary, he can be blamed for always being ready to yield. Even on this question of the succession, the Thembu found him willing and cooperative. He readily agreed and a date was fixed for the visit to Mthatha to advise the government accordingly.

Although abaThembu were aware that the government had recently interfered in the case of amaMpondo after the death of King Mandlonke in 1938, they were not prepared – nor had they considered – the possibility of the government opposing their decision. They had fondly imagined their appointment with the magistrate was just a formality. On the day of the visit to Mthatha, they were in high spirits, which were not dampened even when the magistrate asked them questions about their heir, which they thought were irrelevant and inconsequential.

They held their tempers and showed commendable forbearance and patience, as the magistrate asked them for the heir's date of birth, his birth certificate, his baptismal certificate, his educational certificates and what standard he had passed. To them, all this was stalling and provocation or, at best, prevarication and procrastination. They had not brought any certificates; they were convinced he was just being difficult if not insolent. What would the certificate prove? If the birth certificate was not available, did it really matter? The Thembu delegation returned home, but returned to Mthatha the same week with the birth certificate. They returned home to wait as the magistrate promised to forward everything to the Chief Magistrate who in turn would refer the matter to Pretoria.

When, finally, they were called to Mthatha to hear the government's response, they heaved a sigh of relief, knowing that their long wait was coming to an end. When told that the government believed that the heir had not reached the age of majority and therefore was not ready to succeed his father, you can imagine their stupefaction. To crown it all was the news that the current regent would continue in his post. They managed to control the inward rage they felt as they left dejected and crestfallen. It was unbelievable that the government could stoop so low in its abuse of power and authority.

Although Dabulamanzi had not influenced the government's decision, he was to take the flak. On a point of honour and self-respect, the Thembu felt he should have resigned at that juncture. For him to continue against the firm view and wishes of the people was most insensitive and unwise. From that moment he was regarded as a renegade and stooge. It was Sabata who was to suffer because of this antipathy. Relations between Sabata and the government were bedeviled before Sabata even assumed the reins as sovereign. In its spitefulness and vindictiveness, the government was to delay its approval of Sabata's succession till 1953, when he was 25 years of age.

When the government finally relented and allowed Sabata to assume power as head of the Thembu, it did so grudgingly. There was a strong belief held by government officials that the people leading the movement for the regency's removal were anti-government agitators and malcontents. In the early 1950s, the apartheid government was churning out a plethora of oppressive laws. People in the countryside were restive and resentful of the perceived blatant assault on their diminishing human rights. Under the leadership of the Cape African Teachers' Association, The Society of Young Africa and other bodies all under the umbrella of the All African Convention, an affiliation of the Unity Movement, widespread opposition to the government was mounting.

Chapter 5

Apartheid machinations

Taking advantage of this political ferment, and also the fact that Sabata was now head of the Thembu nation and sympathetic towards his people's aspirations, the Unity Movement activists asked Sabata to host an all-Transkeian meeting to consider the Bantu Education Act, the Bantu Authorities Act and the whole thrust of the government's apartheid policy. All organisations and political formations, as well as the public at large, were invited to this meeting at the Thembu Great Place in December 1954. Support for the meeting was tremendous and from all quarters. All shades of opinion welcomed the opportunity to come together and share views on these burning issues. The turnout exceeded all expectations.

It is a pity good things do not last and quickly get lost. The enthusiasm of the meeting was infectious and the unanimity exhilarating. There was not one dissenting voice. The general feeling of the gathering was aptly put by veteran politico from Xhalanga district, Mr Elijah Qamata, "We must not waste time discussing the pros and cons of these laws. Only a congenital idiot does not see the evil and injustice of these laws and the policy of apartheid. What we should discuss is how to stop the evil and prevent the injustice." The meeting resolved with not one dissenting voice "to reject out of hand both laws and to call upon the people of Transkei to refuse any and all participation in the implementation of these unjust laws".

That was the unequivocal statement from the multitude. When considering the question as to what should be the way forward, the meeting further resolved to send a deputation of four to apprise the government of this decision by the people of Transkei. Members of the delegation were Messrs Elijah Qamata representing Thembuland, C.K. Sakwe of Idutywa representing Gcalekaland (Southern Transkei), Saul Mabude from Mbizana representing Mpondoland and S.S. Majeke from Qumbu representing Mpondomiseland as well as the Bhaca, Xesibe and Embo regions.

The four members of the deputation were all seasoned veterans with wide experience and a long track record of political activity, particularly the first three. They were respected seniors and the backbone of the United Transkeian Territories General Council (Bhunga), where they were also in the executive, even though they had sullied their reputations by becoming members of the emasculated Natives'

Representative Council. They had, thus, in the process, misled and deceived the people that membership of that supine body was worthwhile and in the best interests of the African Community. For all that, they were still held in high regard both for their vast experience and knowledge, as well as their capability. The fourth, S.S. Majeke, while not in the same category and belonging to a younger generation, was an up-and-coming rising star in the political firmament in Transkei and a likely successor to the Sakwes and Qamatas.

Political pundits were anticipating a spectacle when these trusted and dignified Bhunga stalwarts were to turn up in Pretoria as a delegation from Transkei. They imagined that they would present their manifesto "rejecting *in toto*" Acts of the South African parliament and declaring "refusal to participate in the implementation of those unjust laws" to surprised and baffled Bantu Affairs officials. These Bhunga councillors were better known for their unenviable role of presenting to the people unwelcome and unwanted government measures. Now it was hoped the tables would be turned against the government. Officials would be told to their faces that the people of Transkei were telling them and their government "to go to hell".

However, that is not how the sequence of events turned out. The deputation duly *notified* the Deputy Secretary of Bantu Affairs, Bruce Young, of their impending trip to Pretoria and the purpose thereof. They had chosen to refer the matter to him because the latter was a Transkeian and his father, Mould Young, had been Chief Magistrate of Transkei with the sobriquet "Zithulele" (the placid). Bruce Young was a "homeboy". The Secretary was Dr W.W.M. Eiselen, one of the architects and theoreticians of apartheid. They did not wish to attempt to beard the lion in its own den.

In Pretoria, the deputation was to find that senior government officials were not prepared "to put up with any nonsense from cheeky or uppity natives". As a result, the deputation was not met by the deputy secretary or by any other senior member of government, but by a junior clerk who gave them a dressing down, "I am deeply shocked and disappointed at your poor behaviour. You came here to defy the government, what cheek! You bring a paper repudiating laws passed by the South African parliament. Your actions, as you are well aware, are treasonable. You are people who should know better, as senior Bhunga members. I am not accepting your rude manifesto. Mr Bruce Young will not see you."

"What you have done", continued the junior clerk, "is completely out of character and no one would expect this from you. As Bhunga members you have always been dignified and respectful in your approach. In turn, the government has always valued your advice and has always been ready to listen. It seems you have allowed yourselves to be used by agitators and rabble-rousers. Anyway, you have wasted your time and money by coming here. Nobody is going to listen to you. Go home, think clearly and see where you have erred. When you have come to your senses and can see clearly, you will come up with something better than this insolent stuff. You know the well-tried Bhunga ways. You express your loyalty to the government. You do not challenge or confront the government. You accept the law the government has made in its wisdom and you humbly request the government to make suitable amendments here and there. You will find the government is ready to listen. Now go home and do not get into trouble."

With that, the junior clerk showed them out and they left with their tails between their legs. They had not been given a chance to put a word in edgeways. That is about all we were able to glean from second-hand sources. The four never came back to report to the meeting.

If the delegation achieved anything, it was to make the government aware of the overwhelming and widespread opposition to its apartheid policy and the two laws: the Bantu Authorities Act and Bantu Education Act. They decided on a propaganda campaign to blunt opposition and to cajole and win adherents. That was how the government was forced to bring in a new type of propaganda official, named "information officers", countrywide. These officers were better paid than ordinary civil servants and were trained to lie with straight faces. The government's success, however, was not due to the efficacy of paid liars, but to its crackdown on all opposition. It was the efficiency of the Police State and its ruthlessness that enabled the government to enforce and carry on with its inhumane policy.

In 1955, the government commenced its crackdown on the CATA with its massive dismissals of teachers. CATA had been campaigning against Bantu Education and Bantu Authorities, and in so doing, they had defied the government and undermined its policy. The government was able to dismiss scores of teachers with no visible reaction from the African community.

It was apparent the teachers' association was far ahead of the general populace. There were no demonstrations, nor protests. Instead, there was criticism of the teachers for openly showing their political colours. Some critics went further and said the teachers, as civil servants, should have known better. Civil servants could not take up an anti-government position. It was apparent education was not a favourable terrain for challenging the government.

When the government in one fell swoop dismissed the whole executive of CATA and many members of the organisation, it crippled not just the teachers and their organisation, but the liberatory struggle as a whole. In Transkei, in particular, the blow was devastating. For the record, it must be stated that first and foremost, these CATA stalwarts were studious and conscientious teachers. CATA President, Mr Nathaniel Honono, was a good example of this: Nqabara Secondary School in Willowvale District had been opened as the first secondary school in the rural areas amidst a lot of misgivings and pessimism. As principal, "Tshutsha", as Mr Honono was fondly called, evinced such commitment and dedication that he was able to raise the school to such a high level that its pupils' results could compete favourably with established and renowned schools such as Lovedale, Healdtown and St John's College.

It can thus be said that CATA members and the leadership were not just vociferous agitators who neglected their duties and sacrificed the interests of the child. Their talents and excellence were not confined to the classroom.

It was the Mpondo chief, Botha Sigcau, who was the first to break the ranks and breach the resolutions of the Bumbane meeting of 1954. His secretary was Mr Saul Mabude, one of the delegation who had been sent to Pretoria. A report came through the media that Eastern Mpondoland had accepted the Bantu Authorities Act and a Qawukeni Regional Authority would be established, together with the district authorities for the four districts Mbizana, Flagstaff, Lusikisiki and Ntabankulu. It was also revealed that the Mpondo monarch had obtained a concession, giving him power to appoint the Chairman of each district authority.

Chapter 6

AmaMpondo

The case of Mpondoland calls for some expatiation. Although amaMpondo had made some dubious decisions in the past (there are examples of collaboration with colonisers and imperialists), on the whole, amaMpondo cannot correctly be referred to as having been "good native boys".

In fact, they had not agreed to annexation, but had opted for protectorate status when they realised that their territory was coveted by both Natal and the Cape Colony. Faced with the danger of attack by the Cape, they entered into what they believed were negotiations for protectorate status. They were outwitted because they negotiated with the officials of the Cape government and not with the British government directly and discovered they had been annexed to the Cape Colony in 1897. This had rankled with the amaMpondo ever since and throughout the early 20th century, the government was at pains to nurse Mpondo susceptibilities. Until the death of Marhelane in 1918, no Mpondo monarch had ever set foot at the Magistrate's office. It was the magistrate who had to go to Qawukeni if he wanted to do business with the Mpondo monarch. The death of Mandlonke in 1938 opened the way and the government seized the long sought-after opportunity to meddle in and interfere directly in Mpondo affairs.

Mandlonke had a very short time as Mpondo sovereign until his untimely death in 1938. He was already married, but had no male issue yet. He had several half-brothers, including Botha Sigcau, who was chief at Ntlenzi in the Flagstaff District. The other was Nelson, who was still a student at Adam's College in KwaZulu Natal. Before the question of succession was decided, one Singethem Dindi from the royal house at Qawukeni was appointed regent. The Lusikisiki magistrate called a meeting which was well attended and said that on behalf of the government, he wanted clarity on three issues.

The first was whether the late Mandlonke had left any male issue and, if so, who? Secondly, if the late monarch had more than one issue, which of them was heir according to custom? If Mandlonke had no male issue, which of his brothers was highest in rank and would be the putative heir? During the event and in answer to the magistrate, an Mpondo spokesman opined, "Mandlonke left no male issue and no brother in his mother's house. The brother who is to succeed is therefore found in the junior house and is Nelson." The magistrate asked if there was a seconder and a seconder obliged.

All these questions caused no disquiet among the Mpondo and appeared to be innocent inquiry. It was only much later when it was discovered that the magistrate had an axe to grind. It is said that the government already favoured Chief Botha Sigcau of Ntlenzi, who had been found to be pliable and submissive

The Mpondo chiefs present thought the magistrate had obtained the information required and the business was over. To their surprise and puzzlement, the magistrate went on, "Is any other name put forward?" One headman stood up and said "Botha Sigcau". The magistrate asked if there was a seconder. There was rowdiness and commotion and the regent appealed for order and calm. He then said to the magistrate gently, "You are the one who is going off course and causing the trouble. I can see you are thinking of a vote. We are not dealing with headmen here, where the matter is decided by vote. These are chiefs and in chieftainship, it is custom that rules. There is no question of a vote or choice as to whom one prefers."

The magistrate interrupted saying, "I do not need nor want a lecture. I had called for a seconder, is there a seconder?" Someone got up to second Botha's nomination. The magistrate called for those supporting Botha to show their hands. The numbers are not readily available, but it is said that the number was paltry as only two chiefs and their followers supported Botha. The support for Nelson was an overwhelming 99,9% of the meeting, but they refused to vote, saying they would not allow the magistrate to mislead them. Thus it was that the magistrate in his report gave the numbers who voted for Botha, few as they were. Crucially, he recorded that nobody had voted for Nelson.

The events of that day are still a talking point, even today. Some have faulted the supporters of Nelson for obstinacy and inflexibility. Others have argued that Nelson's supporters were correct in principle, but unwise tactically. It is said all of Lusikisiki, Ntabankulu and Mbizana were for Nelson. In Flagstaff, except for the two Administrative Areas under chiefs Lumayi Langa and Nobulongwe Masiphula, supported Botha's candidacy. All the others, the preponderant majority, were for Nelson. Without that initial tactical advantage, Botha was a non-starter as Nelson was leading by the proverbial mile. AmaMpondo tried hard to undo the mischief that had been caused on that fateful day, but were never able to get things right again. However, that is not the kernel of our story. That was just by-the-by. Botha was duly installed as Mpondo monarch and the Mpondo will was thwarted.

The Mpondo monarch was not to have an easy ride on the Bantu Authorities coach. His first troubles were to come from Ntabankulu. Even before Bantu Authorities, Botha had had a close brush with death. In Lusikisiki district, there is an area bordering the sea called Mantusini. It is wooded country, a large portion of which had been demarcated as forestland although it was inhabited and contained many households. It would appear the government had hoped gradually to rid the demarcated forestland of households. The procedure followed for years was that when a householder died, his son would be required to move. Evidently there had been laxity and instead of decreasing, the numbers of householders had increased.

When Mr Leppan arrived as magistrate, he wanted to put the matter right once and for all. He gave instructions that the occupiers of land in the forest area should find sites elsewhere and gave them 12 months to do so. When people learnt that they had been given an "ultimatum" to get out of the area in 12 months, they were furious. To the best of their knowledge and belief, their expulsion from the forest area had been abandoned long before and was defunct. Why this busybody was resurrecting something that had died a natural death a long time before, they could not fathom. In any event, the people of Mantusini were prepared to resist and determined to stay, believing Leppan would give up. One of their chief spokesmen and the man the authorities said was the ring-leader, was Mngqingo Phicani. Because of his uncompromising stand and forceful delivery, he had become the leader.

When Leppan realised the opposition was gathering momentum and showed signs of an incipient rebellion, he decided to adopt pacifying moves. He asked for a meeting with the Mantusini residents to discuss and resolve the impasse amicably. He was warned it would be dangerous for him to visit the area because of inflamed passions and, as a precaution, asked the Mpondo Paramount Chief Botha Sigcau to be present at the proposed meeting. It was this foresight that saved their lives. The Mantusini residents had decided to put an end to the land dispute drastically, that is, by killing the magistrate and his party. They did not know the Paramount had been invited to attend and would be present at the meeting. Botha's unexpected arrival at the meeting necessitated a quick rethink.

On that fateful day, Leppan was already seated, with the Mpondo monarch next to him. The meeting was about to commence when some amaMpondo chanted a song. Others joined and then about six, brandishing sticks, came to the open area in front of the table facing the magistrate. The singing was more like a war cry and the six simulated a charge and again retreated brandishing sticks menacingly. The situation was becoming charged and suddenly Mngqingo took the stage and upbraided Leppan for his determination to uproot people.

As he spoke, one man was performing a dance routine. He concluded his dance by turning round, lifting up his leather kilt and then obscenely bending and opening his backside with both hands to Leppan. Mngqingo stopped his denouncement and dismissed the gathering and then added, "To our horses! Let us saddle and go!" As the throng followed Mngqingo, Leppan used that opportunity to make a swift getaway.

The story goes thus. The arrival and the presence of the Mpondo monarch had upset the plans of the Mantusini people. The leaders had quickly huddled together in a hut to debate what to do in the circumstances. Some were saying in anger and desperation, "We can't change our plans, we will just kill Botha as well. We won't allow his unasked presence to foil our plans." Mngqingo pleaded, "No, no, no, not Botha! We would be inviting all Mpondoland to wipe us out! Just imagine the war cry, 'The Mantusini has murdered the king!' We would have no place to hide." He was still busy with his persuasion when someone came into the hut and announced, "Things are getting out of hand outside!" It was this that made Mngqingo dash outside to take charge to prevent a disaster.

Of course, to Leppan and company, Mngqingo was not their saviour, but the man who nearly caused their death. He was arrested, charged, convicted and sentenced to nine months' imprisonment. After his release from jail, he was banished and removed to the Northern Transvaal. His case was full of drama and he was ably represented by Attorney J.G.S. Vabaza of Libode. Dubul'ekhephuza, as Vabaza was fondly called, used to say he realised from the start he would not win the case, but was determined not to adopt the tempting approach of appeasement, which was to plead guilty and show remorse. His client was in a combative mood, not repentant, nor hoping for the mercy of the court. Vabaza knew that if he won the jousting in the courtroom, he would have earned his money regardless of any verdict or sentence.

At Mantusini, Paramount Chief Botha Sigcau had not uttered a word and it was not necessary. As Leppan himself had expected, as the Mpondo monarch, the aura of his presence was sufficient to protect him and ensure that no one came to harm. What a pity the ravages of conquest, colonialism/imperialism, have eroded this treasure. It is only fair to add that examples abound where our own royalty has been guilty of plain stupidity and even betrayal, thus squandering this goodwill.

Did Botha learn any lessons from the Mantusini faux pas? It would appear not and he was blindly proceeding from one blunder to the next. In its callousness and cynicism the government wanted to use Paramount Chief Botha in the case against Mngqingo and poor Botha was a willing and unwitting tool. He was being made complainant in the case, instead of Leppan. If the government wished to charge Mngqingo, that was their affair, and Botha should not have allowed the traduce of his name or to be used against his people. Botha had his own court and could summon Mngqingo to his court if he felt Mngqingo had committed any transgression.

What is more, the Mantusini meeting was not Botha's. It had been called by the magistrate and Botha had merely been invited to attend. In any event, the shortsighted, unsuspecting Botha attended court at Lusikisiki as complainant. Mngqingo was charged with disturbing or breaking up a meeting of Paramount Chief Botha Sigcau and also showing disrespect to the said chief. The magistrate was being shielded from the rough-and-tumble of cross examination and was not even listed as a witness. It was Botha they would use as a pawn in the game. The case attracted vast crowds and was a spectacular show.

In his cross examination of the complainant, the Mpondo Paramount Botha, Dubul'ekhephuza was merciless and relentless. Botha was to confide to his closest friends that the torment he went through was one of the worst experiences of his life. He felt that Vabaza was hitting him below the belt when he baited him about being a chief duly appointed under the Native Administration Act No. 38 of 1927. It was a hard one for Chief Botha to swallow that he was not a chief by virtue of Pondo Law and custom. Vabaza seemed to be highlighting his illegitimacy that he was not a chief by birth and of right, but on the strength of White government appointment and Botha had had to concede.

He was grilled about his presence at the meeting, "Did you call the meeting? Were you a participant or just an invited guest? At whose instance did you attend? What was the purpose of your visit? Were you aware of the land dispute? Were you joining the land dispute? Were Mngqingo's remarks directed at you?" The barrage of questions left him physically, mentally and emotionally exhausted. His dignity and respectability had been left in tatters. Unfortunately, he did not draw the correct conclusions and accept blame for acting unwisely. He believed Vabaza did not handle him with due respect and consideration and had been especially cruel.

Chapter 7

The Mpondo succession

We come now to Botha's acceptance of Bantu Authorities. The Mantusini experience was already a thing of the past and was becoming just a bad memory.

In the way he used the concession he had obtained, of nominating the head of the district authority, Botha was to cause himself many headaches in the district of Ntabankulu. The Cwerha are the predominant tribal group there and are spread over a big area comprising many administrative areas under the collective Cwerhaland. However, according to their origin and classification, they belong to amaMpondomise. Because they were not "true" Mpondo, the appointment of a Cwerha as head of the district authority would give them additional clout. Botha decided to bypass them. The senior Mpondo Chief in the district was Zibulele Ndamase of Mangqamzeni, a man of stature; well-educated, knowledgeable, financially sound and one of the pillars in the political and social life of the Transkei. Unfortunately, genealogically he belonged to the Nyandeni Mpondo. Botha felt Zibuzele ought to be cut down to size and not given a further boost. He too was bypassed.

Finally, the Mpondo monarch opted to appoint one Madlanya Thantsi. Most people were shocked and puzzled by this choice. In its propaganda campaign, the government had been harping on the point that Bantu Authorities restored the inherent and traditional power of the chiefs and the authority of the nation. Now Madlanya was just a headman and there were several chiefs in the district. What is more, Madlanya was under the senior Mpondo Chief in the district who was Zibuzele Ndamase. To confound them further was the fact that although belonging to the Mpondo royal clan, Nyawuza, Madlanya was not a descendant of the Great Faku. Madlanya's appointment seemed to negate the supposed purpose of Bantu Authorities and ran counter to its publicised aims.

Chief Zibuzele sent a deputation to Qawukeni to persuade the monarch to correct this "inadvertent error". Paramount Botha refused to budge and to rescind Madlanya's appointment. The Mangqamzeni deputation was then sent to the Chief Magistrate in Mthatha, requesting him to intervene and redress the injustice. The Chief Magistrate would not assist them. He did not see his way clear to interfere with Paramount Botha in the lawful exercise of the latter's prerogative. He advised them to go back to Qawukeni with their grievances. It seemed they had come to a dead end. Chief Zibuzele had accepted the Bantu Authorities, but now he found the process stifling and suffocating.

Fortunately, Chief Zibuzele had several business interests and he decided the time had come for him to devote more time to his business affairs. He notified the Mangqamzeni people that he was relinquishing the Chieftainship, but as his son was still a minor, he was appointing someone to act as regent during the heir's minority. In reply, his councillors agreed his position had become untenable and they regretfully accepted his decision to step down. They did not agree with his choice of regent, however, and thought he was making the same mistake Paramount Botha had made. In their respectful submission, they said regency was governed by and should follow custom. In the Mangqamzeni hierarchy, his younger brother, Notseke, was the highest below him and it was thus unacceptable to bypass Notseke and place over the nation and over Notseke an underling. Surprisingly, it was the turn of Chief Zibuzele to show the obstinacy they had encountered at Qawukeni. He would not listen to his councillors and refused to appoint Notseke.

From initially organising to oppose Chief Zibuzele on his choice of regent, the councillors' campaign grew and expanded to rejecting Bantu Authorities, the Bantustan policy and the government policy of apartheid – and also led to their involvement in the peasant revolt of 1960 (cf: which at the time was happening in the Belgian Congo, with Patrice Lumumba and the Congolese people rising in revolt against Belgian colonial rule).

We end our sojourn to Mpondoland and in the next chapter, return our focus to Thembuland, to examine how the Thembu performance compares to the Pondo.

Chapter 8

The rise of K.D. (Kaiser) Matanzima

It had been government strategy to tackle Mpondoland first and, with that safely in the bag, the government did not find it difficult to pressure the other nations to follow suit. The domino effect continued as area after area fell into the government trap. The one and only exception was Thembuland, which stood fast and unshaken in its resolve to have nothing to do with the abominable system put in place by the government.

White supremacists strongly believed in their innate superiority and had unshakable confidence in the venality of the African. They believed that every native had a price and it was just a matter of finding the right price. The government now turned its attention to the Thembu sovereign, Sabata, to try and find out what price they would have to pay for his co-operation. The fat prize they decided to dangle before him was the return and re-incorporation of the Glen Grey district to Thembuland. This was a matter the Chief Magistrate would handle himself, because of its importance and sensitivity.

When Sabata was requested to call at the Chief Magistrate's office at his earliest convenience, he did not know what to expect. He found the Chief Magistrate, J.J. Yates, in an amicable mood and, although Sabata was initially suspicious and wary, in due course he felt at ease and relaxed. Over tea and during preliminary conversation, the Chief Magistrate spoke of the cordial relations between the government and the Thembu nation. He recounted the long history of interaction from the days of Ngangelizwe and stressed the mutual benefits to both sides.

When they came to the business in hand, the Chief Magistrate prefaced his message with the remark that the government wished and preferred to work with King Sabata. In its desire to restore the dignity of the people and chiefs, the government recognised the importance of working closely with the chiefs, the traditional leaders. In the case of the Thembu it meant working with the king. He said he wished to talk about the Glen Grey district, which was an integral part of Thembuland. The government was ready to return the territory to Thembuland as part of its project for greater Thembuland with seven districts compared to the present six. Before embarking on the project, the government wanted to be assured of the readiness on Sabata's part to co-operate with the government. He, Yates, favoured entrusting to Sabata the question of persuading the people of Glen Grey on this matter of re-incorporation. Sabata would gain the credit for this and it would raise his stature and popularity. The Chief Magistrate said he was aware of King Sabata's reluctance to accept Bantu Authorities, but wished to assure him that he had nothing to lose but much to gain. He did not want to rush him and would give him two weeks to think the matter over.

Two weeks is a short time and, on its expiry, the sovereign was back at the Chief Magistrate's office. The Chief Magistrate was visibly disappointed and unhappy as he listened to the sovereign explain his predicament. He implored the Chief Magistrate to understand that the Thembu people were truly against the Bantu Authorities Act and he was, and had to be, with his people. The Chief Magistrate teased him by saying it appeared he was acting more like the tail and not the head. When he realised the sovereign was resolute in his stand he uttered ominous words, warning Sabata that he was forcing the government to look for someone else to work with. Yates said he dreaded the disastrous consequences for King Sabata if that were to happen. Anyway, he said, the sovereign had been given the opportunity, but had chosen not to take it.

Even as the two parted, the government was already busy looking for someone to work for it, to implement the apartheid measures. All six magistrates in Thembuland had been given instructions to do all in their power to undermine the sovereign and break the unity of abaThembu. Mr J.D. Cornell, magistrate at Engcobo, did not succeed in cajoling the Qwati, the big tribe in Ngcobo, nor did Mr T.D. Young of Mqanduli manage to win the amaQiha or other small tribes at Mqanduli. It was Mr Fenwick of Elliotdale who was to register the first success, when he prevailed upon Chief Zwelenqaba and his Bomvana tribe to pass a resolution renouncing any allegiance to or membership of abaThembu, and requesting re-incorporation to amaGcalekas under King Zwelidumile of the Xhosas.

While abaThembu were still reeling under the shock of the Bomvana secession and making frantic efforts to challenge the legality of the secession, bad news came from inside Thembuland proper. The disturbing report came that Chief K.D. Matanzima had accepted the Bantu Authorities Act and that, consequently, a tribal authority would be installed at Qamata, shortly. Now this was something very serious, for it was not some obscure chieftain doing mischief. Chief Matanzima was a bona fide member of the Thembu royal house and a senior besides. Because of his academic accomplishments, he was held in high esteem. It was unthinkable that he of all people could be guilty of disloyal – even treasonable – conduct. AbaThembu were appalled and disgusted.

What had happened? How could it be that the likeable K.D. Matanzima had become a transgressor? Truth is stranger than fiction, we have been told many times, but the truth still manages to surprise us repeatedly. The true story is that that same Bruce Young, the Under Secretary who had declined to see the Transkei deputation in Pretoria, was responsible for K.D.'s defection from Thembu-adherent, to becoming a government devotee. Evidently Mr Young had done his homework and had spotted the Achilles heel among those opposing the government. He came to Mthatha and requested that K.D. be brought to Mthatha for talks. The parties involved have as yet not breached the confidentiality of the talks. However, our trusted informant from the Chief Magistrate's office, Mr Hulley Mgudlwa himself, leaked the gist of the talks.

It is said Bruce Young's gambit was to remind K.D. of his request for a salary raise, which had not succeeded. He also reminded him of his longing for jurisdiction to hear cases at Qamata. He then pointed out how the Bantu Authorities answered both requests favourably. Of course, we do not know all that was actually said, but we do know that K.D. left Mthatha convinced the apartheid government offered him much that he desired. He was lost to the Thembu cause from then onward and the apartheid regime never found a more devoted and faithful servant.

AbaThembu were furious and Sabata's councillors were itching to teach K.D. a lesson he would not forget. K.D. was summoned to appear at Bumbane, but instead, he reported to the Cofimvaba magistrate, Mr D.J.M. Jordaan, who told him to ignore the summons and that the government would deal with the Thembu king. The sovereign was called to Mthatha and given "friendly advice" by the Chief Magistrate to "leave K.D. alone". The aggrieved Sabata argued strenuously, but in vain that, as Thembu supremo, he was responsible for the whole of Thembuland. He said his surveillance over subordinate chiefs, including Matanzima, was a domestic Thembu affair which did not require government interference. The government had its way, however, and thus prevented Sabata from disciplining K.D.

A precedent had been set and, from then on K.D., felt free to flout decisions and orders from Bumbane. If anything, this caused confusion and potential conflict. After the Qamata Tribal Authority was established, and before the year was out, the St Mark's District Authority came into being with K.D. Matanzima as Chairman. That now threw the whole district into turmoil. To K.D., his position of Chairman of the district authority meant he was senior to all chiefs in the district, with power to bring them all to his court at Qamata. In alarm, Chief Qaqawuli Mgudlwa of the Jumba at Qhumanco, and Chief Zwelakhe Ndarhala of the Ndungwane at Banzi, asked the magistrate to intervene. The magistrate declined, informing them it would be improper for him to meddle in Bantu Authorities affairs.

Chief Qaqawuli took his complaint to the Thembu sovereign and Sabata summoned K.D. Matanzima and Qaqawuli to appear before him at Bumbane. Yet again the government interfered and instructed the Thembu sovereign to back off and leave Matanzima alone. This time, the flimsy pretext was that as Sabata had not accepted Bantu Authorities, he had no right or power to adjudicate in Bantu Authorities disputes. The sovereign tried in vain to explain that this was a simple case of a misunderstanding between two of his subordinate chiefs. Again the sovereign was overruled. The result was that Chief Qaqawuli decided to relinquish his chieftainship. He refused to be the first Jumba Chief to subject himself to K.D. Matanzima, chief of the Hala, his equal in rank.

That was just the beginning of the troubles in the district of St Mark's as K.D. flexed his muscles, and – against much resistance – was spreading his tentacles far and wide throughout the district. The sovereign had his hands full, resolving dispute after dispute as there was a constant flow of complaints against K.D.'s excesses and exactions. In effect, the sovereign was continuously untying all the knots K.D. was making. However, the government always took sides with K.D. against his sovereign. In an attempt to solve "the bad working relations between the two", the Chief Magistrate advised the sovereign to work *through* Matanzima, that is, to use Matanzima and not act in parallel with him. He used the example that he, as Chief Magistrate, did not visit a district without agreement with the district magistrate. As K.D. was his (the sovereign's) local representative, the sovereign ought to delegate district matters to K.D. and not bypass him or attend to them personally.

Half-heartedly at first, K.D. came up with a new complaint. He said the sovereign was not giving him scope and space to operate. He quoted the examples of amaGcaleka and amaRharhabe, saying amaRharhabe were given full latitude south of the Kei. He also referred to the amaMpondo, saying a similar situation existed in Mpondoland in that the Ndamases at Nyandeni were to all intents and purposes in full control. He said he felt the same should apply to the St Mark's district. As he grew bolder and more confident in his claim, he complained that he had been deprived of this right by the sovereign who wanted everything for himself. Of course, this was a blatant lie.

The situation was not static and the St Mark's district was dividing into pro-Sabata and pro-Matanzima factions. To give a boost to Chief Matanzima, and hopefully gain advantage for him over the sovereign in the increasing rivalry, the government launched development projects in the district of St Mark's. An irrigation scheme to ensure year-round crop-raising was put in place and the Qamata Dam was built. Dams, clinics, windmills, etc. became available when in the rest of the country such facilities were a rarity. The monarch's visits and surveillance were a constant worry to K.D. and the government. Something had to be done to give Chief Matanzima free, unfettered rein and keep Sabata out.

It was in this climate that Thembuland in 1958 received news of a pending commission (the Bruce Young Commission) to investigate the continuing unrest in Thembuland and its causes, as well as the validity of the claim by Kaiser Matanzima to Paramountcy in "Western" Thembuland and to determine the area involved. When abaThembu were invited to come and testify before the Bruce Young Commission, the consensus of opinion was:

1. They did not want any commission and felt there was no need for one.
2. What did the government want to find out, which it did not know already?
3. This was a ploy in some government agenda whose real purpose the people could not fathom.
4. The government's intentions were not good and the commission should be shunned.

As a precaution, the Thembu king sought legal advice on how to handle the situation. Just in case, a memorandum was prepared stating the Thembu view on the commission itself, as well as a response to K.D. Matanzima's spurious claim of the existence of two Thembulands. There was no unanimity as to what strategy to follow. The suggestion to boycott the commission, although enjoying strong support, was rejected by many as tactically unwise and self-defeating. It was also unclear whether by attending, abaThembu would be compromised and find themselves lending credibility to the government's shady manoeuvres. Up to the day of the commission, there was still no certainty about what abaThembu would do.

It was agreed nonetheless that they should come to Mthatha in their thousands in a show of force and solidarity with the sovereign, in the face of K.D.'s disloyalty.

AbaThembu were correct in regarding the commission with suspicion, although they did not have knowledge of the facts or reasons for the government's decision. The sovereign's strength and popularity were based on the openness of his court and the full participation of the rank-and-file peasantry in decisions taken. It was this court that produced the councillors who were the dominant feature of his rule. The Thembu Secretary, Bhalisile Nkosiyane, was *de facto* chief of staff. Recruited from the government service, he performed his duties with competence and diligence.

He had a full dossier about the government's machinations and chicanery. He was to astound and confound the commission with his disclosures. On the morning of the commission, abaThembu descended on Mthatha in their thousands, in a show of support and solidarity with their beleaguered monarch. They camped on the south-western end of the commonage, the present Fort Gale. When the stated starting time was approaching, messengers were dispatched to the Bhunga building, the venue, to advise that the Thembu and their king were ready for the commission at the commonage. The reply from Mr Bruce Young was that abaThembu should come down to town as the commission could not sit in the veld.

Messengers went to and fro and it was abaThembu who finally yielded. The monarch went to the Bhunga building to take part in the commission along with a retinue of 30 councillors. The presentation of abaThembu was forthright, incisive and to the point. The so-called unrest in Thembuland was fomented by the government and its officials. It was the direct result of the government's fixation in sponsoring, nurturing and foisting the unwanted Matanzima as the government tool in the breaking up of Thembuland. There was one Thembuland and one monarch. The government was wrong in defying abaThembu by trying to create another Thembuland for Matanzima, outside the authority of the sovereign, Sabata. It was government meddling that was the source and cause of the unrest. The charges against the government were fully documented.

The Thembu Secretary, Nkosiyane, was guilty of unpardonable sin in the eyes of the government. He had the audacity to quote from official government correspondence to expose government duplicity. On the issue of Elliotdale and its secession, he produced correspondence exposing Mr Fenwick's complicity. It revealed that Fenwick was the author and driver of the Bomvana move. In the case of K.D., again, he produced correspondence between the Cofimvaba magistrate and the Chief Magistrate. From the correspondence, it was clear for all to see that the government and Matanzima were working together and the government was the driving force behind their collusion. For his temerity of throwing stolen government correspondence in the face of the commission, he could not be pardoned.

The contribution by Bangilizwe Joyi and his cousin, Twalimfene Joyi, concentrated on Thembu law and custom. They also dealt with proper channels and procedures. They averred it was abaThembu who knew best who K.D. was and what his position in the Thembu hierarchy was. If K.D. felt aggrieved, he should have referred the matter to the Thembu Court and he had not done so. K.D. was a member of the Thembu royal house and the Dlomo clan would be his first point of call if K.D. had a grievance. K.D. was also a qualified lawyer and had not brought a case before any court of law. If one had no valid case, was it permissible and proper to hold a commission to create a case for him? Who had requested this commission?

Macgregor Mgolombane said to the best of his knowledge and belief that K.D.'s position and status was the same as his father Mhlobo, Mhlobo's was the same as *his* father Mvuzo's, and Mvuzo's the same as *his* father Matanzima's. He continued by asking questions. Why must the commission come to disturb the status quo? If there was nothing wrong in the position and status of K.D.'s forebears, what was the ground or basis for thinking there was just cause to look into the matter? What wrong did the commission wish to correct? The commission should not waste time and money. It should pack up and go, and report everything was in order in Thembuland, except for the mischief caused by government officials.

The commission finished its sitting and, after two weeks, the government commenced its vicious assault on abaThembu. The four leading spokesmen, Messers J.B. Nkosiyane, Bangilizwe Joyi, Twalimfene Joyi and MacGregor Mgolombane were served with banishment orders sending them to far-flung parts of South Africa, mostly in the Northern Transvaal. Even for South Africa, with its long record of injustice and iniquity, this turn of events was unexpected. In its cynical contempt for all civilised norms and standards, the apartheid government was now punishing people for testifying before a government commission.

The Thembu sovereign relied on and trusted his councillors. As he was often to observe, it was best if the people themselves were the ones who took decisions on all matters affecting them. He steadfastly refused to accept any measure or proposal from the government. Everything had to be referred to "ibandla", that is, the general public meeting. He often prefaced his remarks with the observation, "Everything must be referred to the people. If it is a good thing, they will reap the fruits and, vice versa. If it is a bad thing, they are the ones who will suffer the evil consequences thereof."

He prided himself on the good fortune that he had knowledgeable and honest councillors. He assured the people that their well-meant advice would never fall on deaf ears. He said he was determined never to disappoint them and he believed the Thembu masses would never let him down. In rejecting apartheid and its measures like Bantu Authorities, he claimed he was following the will of the people. However, a close scrutiny of his approach and actions shows that he himself found the policy repulsive and abhorrent.

In dealings with the government and its officials, he didn't have to be candid and say so openly. It was sensible and discreet merely to plead that, as sovereign, he was and had to be with the people. He had no separate or private agenda apart from what is usually referred to as the reasonable wants and wishes of the people themselves. He was there to promote *their* welfare and not his own selfish interests.

What about the head of the commission, Bruce Young? With his position as Deputy Secretary and therefore head of Bantu Administration, how could he be a member – let alone head – of a commission investigating matters in his department? With his history and personal association with and involvement in K.D.'s appointment and affairs in general, common decency should have told him to recuse himself. With no conscience or scruple, he coolly headed a commission that required impartiality and objectivity. As we were to discover *post facto*, the so-called commission was no commission at all. It was all bluff.

The whole exercise was a charade. This was part of the build-up of putting K.D. in line with the government's Bantustan scheme. It was not for abaThembu of Transkei, but for the broader South African constituency. They were the ones to swallow the bluff that K.D. had not just been hand-picked and had Paramountcy bestowed upon him. They needed the assurance that a genuine commission had, after proper enquiry, established the validity of his Paramountcy. They were not to know that the matter had been decided beforehand, and that in coming to Mthatha and heading the sittings, Bruce Young was merely going through the motions. They did not know that, if Bruce Young had any self-respect, there would have been no Bruce Young Commission. Neither were they to know that the testimony before him fell on deaf ears and was completely disregarded when making his findings. There is no gainsaying the fact that the submissions by the Thembu spokesmen were both unchallengeable and unanswerable.

It is thus apparent that part of Bruce Young's agenda was to find out who the stalwarts were in the forces opposing the government. Having discovered them, the government did not hesitate to banish them forthwith. With its undisguised contempt for the African, there was no need to explain its actions. The story goes that the government had seriously considered banishing the Thembu sovereign himself. It only refrained from this dastardly step when warned that if their dirty hands touched the king, Matanzima would not last 24 hours. The converse was also true. On many occasions, one or other patriot vexed to the limit by Matanzima's betrayal, had resolved to kill K.D. Always, cool heads had prevailed and the would-be assassin would be reprimanded. "No, don't, the sovereign would get the flack. Don't expose him to unnecessary jeopardy." So fear of danger to one ensured the safety of the other and that was to continue for years.

Defying all opposition, the government was proceeding unsteadily, but surely towards its stated goals of installing Bantustans for its unwilling "Bantu". Disregarding the current in the rest of the world, that is, the swing towards independence and the liquidation of colonialism, South Africa was moving in reverse and sinking the

African majority deeper into bondage. Judging that the time was ripe to fold up the old Bhunga, the Minister of Bantu Administration and Development, De Wet Nel, came to Mthatha for that purpose. The Bhunga then had to make way for a new institution, viz, Bantu Authorities. De Wet Nel came to Mthatha to wind up the United Transkeian Territories General Council (UTTGC) and to launch the Transkeian Territorial Authority (TTA). He was also to install its Chairman who, by agreement, was to be the Pondo Paramount, Botha Sigcau.

In the now-defunct UTTGC (the Bhunga), people had risen to the top on merit, judged by capability and performance. Thus it was that on important occasions, the Mpondo chief Victor Poto Ndamase had been called upon to act as spokesman. He was chosen not just because of his royal status, but for his sharp intellect, dignified expression, elegance of diction, impressive marshalling of facts, and concise, but pointed delivery. It was the more knowledgeable and articulate individuals who provided the leadership and made up the members of the executive. It appeared that for leadership of the TTA, different criteria applied, namely, royal status only. During the 20 odd years he had attended Bhunga sessions, all the Mpondo Paramount, Botha Sigcau, had done was to keep his seat warm. He had not participated in any debate, not even to say, "I support the motion."

Many in the public gallery of the Bhunga Chambers that day were first-time visitors and the day's events were an eye-opener. De Wet Nel's visit had been publicised as a momentous occasion, the start of the journey towards self-determination. He was coming to officially disband the UTTGC and, in its stead, install the TTA. Not knowing what to expect, all gave the day's events close attention. When Paramount Botha Sigcau commenced his first address as Chairman, there was an air of rapt expectation. What a disappointment it turned out to be!

In his very first sentence, he referred to Nel as "Baas Nel" and the magic spell was broken. People were aghast at this disgusting spectacle, the shameful grovelling from the Chairman and his public avowal that in that gathering, De Wet was "*Baas*". What had all this fuss been about? Of course, there were no boos or catcalls, but the people were stunned. Nobody thought or even imagined that Paramount Sigcau could call anybody "*Baas*".

Chapter 9

Apartheid takes root

The demise of the Bhunga (UTTGC), and the inauguration of the TTA as its successor, together with its Black Chairman, had been touted as the harbinger of a new dawn in South Africa's race relations. As such, the TTA was the beginning of a new process towards the goal of giving the Black majority not just a voice in the running of their own affairs, but eventually full control over their destiny.

The gateway towards this "blissful life" was the Bantu homelands dispensation, for which the TTA was laying the foundation. Such fawning was unheard of even in the Bhunga and Paramount Botha Sigcau's utterance marked a new low. What compounded this ignominy was that there was no correction either by the author (Sigcau) or from the house. It was as if all was in order and business just went on. That in itself spoke volumes about the calibre of its members and its standards. How could any self-respecting assembly find that demeaning utterance acceptable?

One thing is certain: the Mpondo Paramount was not being sarcastic. In his own mind, he was being respectful. He was also showing that he was a "trustworthy and dependable native" (*die goeie kaffir*). He knew his place and accepted that there was no equality between "*Baas*" and "Klaas". This left a bitter taste in the mouth and the sad reflection was that this servility was coming from a person held up to be the head of the Mpondo people.

Paramount Botha Sigcau was one of the so-called traditional leaders who claimed to be the legitimate representative and authentic spokesman of the indigenous population. They were the trusted ones to face up to and challenge Dr H.F. Verwoerd and his Neo-Nazi White supremacists. What a hope! There was no contest. Apartheid had won hands down. One was left pondering the question, "Did this kowtowing reflect poorly on King Botha himself only or was it a shocking revelation of the wretched state of the new body, the TTA, as a whole?"

As later events were to show repeatedly, Botha Sigcau's sickening performance was no blunder, but a graphic pointer of Black South Africa's real status under apartheid. It was at the same time an indicator of the true relationship between the Bantu homelands and the South African government. All these Bantustan structures never rose above that level of abject subservience to their apartheid masters. Not even once did any Bantustan government ever say nay to any dictate of the apartheid regime.

True to its utter contempt for the African, the South African government itself had written the speech which the TTA would deliver in reply to Minister De Wet Nel. Paramount Botha Sigcau was given a preview of the speech. When his councillor Saul Mabude read it, he recoiled in horror at its abject and fawning tone. He advised Paramount Botha Sigcau to give the honour of making the reply to his Deputy, Chief K.D. Matanzima. Thus it was that Chief K.D. Matanzima had the "honour" of reading the degrading speech. He did so with relish and without any qualm, like a good and loyal servant of his apartheid masters. He felt no compunction and, in fact, looked satisfied that he had done a good job.

Later that evening, this author visited Chief K.D. Matanzima at his suite in the local hotel. Driven by the impetuosity of youth, the author blurted out, "I cannot stomach the undisguised contempt these Boers have for you. As for bringing a speech from Pretoria to Mthatha for you to parrot, that is the limit! Why can't you be trusted to say your own thing, your own way?"

From his school days, K.D. was like an elder brother to the author, who felt he could take liberties with him and was not afraid to give vent to his righteous indignation. For all that, the author could not have been prepared for K.D.'s reaction. He was outraged and fumed, "Shame on you! What makes you imagine we are incapable of drafting our own speech? Could it be you supposedly who are the only person with intelligence? If you want to know, that speech was drafted by ourselves in our caucus."

Not realising he had crossed the line, the author went on unwarily, "No, Sir, please, not that one! You cannot be responsible for that abomination. You have your own sins, but not that one." At this juncture, one of the chief's companions, Mr Enoch Tembekile Tshunungwa, observed, "What is this fellow after, is he fishing for trouble?" Realising tempers were getting frayed, and that he had overstepped the mark, the author smiled and politely bade the chief good night and withdrew.

What was contained in the speech brought by De Wet Nel for the TTA to read in reply? The gist was that the people of the Transkei affirmed and wanted the world to know that, of their own accord, they had embraced and accepted the policy of separate development as their own. They also wanted to send a loud and clear message to those nations and individuals who had taken it upon themselves to be the self-appointed spokespersons of the Black people of South Africa, that they had no mandate to speak on their behalf. They also wanted to repudiate the attacks made at the United Nations and other forums castigating the Government of South Africa. They also expressed thanks and gratitude to the South African government for all it was doing to uplift and promote the welfare of the Bantu people.

The salutary lesson one gained from this was that there were all types of people. Some – even in those compromised bodies – were genuine if misguided patriots, hoping and vainly attempting to advance the people's cause. They were shocked at the government's dirty tricks and exposed them. Unfortunately, there were also the dangerous ones who had sold out, body and soul. Instead of exposing the government, they covered up for it. Morally bankrupt, they had lost self-respect and all sense of honour. Even as they masqueraded as leaders, they knew they were nothing more than paid servants of the regime.

Obsequious as they were to their apartheid masters, they were domineering and bullying to their own people. When Dr H.F. Verwoerd was assassinated, Chief K.D. Matanzima moved an unopposed motion of condolence and tribute to the South African Prime Minister. He also called upon Mr Knowledge Guzana, the Opposition Leader in the TTA, to support the motion as a bi-partisan exercise. Although the opposition had not discussed the matter, Mr Guzana surprisingly agreed and associated the opposition with the motion and the sentiments expressed therein.

Dr H.P. Bala, an opposition front-bencher from Butterworth, caught the eye of the Speaker (Mr M. Canca) and was allowed to rise up and speak. He began his address thus. "I have no difficulty with the message of condolence itself, although we in the Opposition have been ambushed. To the tribute, I say NO … " At this point, he was cut short by the Speaker who said the matter had not been opened up for debate and ordered him to sit down. Chief K.D. Matanzima had hurriedly transmitted a message to the Speaker to silence Dr Bala and close the matter.

The Speaker called on the members of the House to stand and observe two minutes' silence in honour of the deceased South African Prime Minister. The House rose, but it was noticed that Dr Bala remained seated. After the two-minute pause, Chief K.D. Matanzima moved that Dr Bala be suspended from the House for two weeks "for unbecoming behaviour in the House". The motion was passed and Dr Bala was sin-binned for two weeks. As Dr Bala later explained to his constituency and friends, he had been defending a point of honour and principle. A tribute is a political statement, and with his abominable track record, Dr H.F. Verwoerd did not deserve any commendation from the African Community.

Perhaps one of the most exasperating features in the dictatorial nature of apartheid was its crude interference in the management and running of people's affairs. In the rural areas, the government had the final word, even in a parochial issue such as who should be headman. It was the government that decided whether or where there should be a clinic. The same; similarly, with the provision of amenities such as windmills, dams and irrigation. The government was also leaning more and more on the chiefs and headmen, requiring them to be the government's eyes and ears. This was creating a dangerous situation; if the chiefs and headmen were compromised and became government spies and informers, it would have dire consequences. While people were prepared to tolerate that unhealthy situation when working in the mines and on White-owned farms, here at home it was just not on.

This is not to say the government was given an easy go. The liberatory movement was active in the field. In the Eastern CATA, the Society of Young Africa, and other organisations affiliated to the All African Convention, were campaigning actively. They were all under the umbrella of the Unity Movement and were projecting a new vision for the country. The Unity Movement with its slogan, "We are building a nation, a non-racial South Africa", was positing the very antithesis to the divisive apartheid. With its emphasis on a principled struggle and its Ten Point Programme to guide and channel its fight for full democratic rights for all, it was blazing a new trail. Its policy of no compromise with the oppressor, as well as no collaboration in the working of oppressive laws, guarded against opportunism. In its arsenal, the use of the boycott was a powerful weapon. The strategy was not complicated.

Chapter 10

The people's response

One thing the African masses were never happy with was the appellation "non-European" and its negative connotation. Colonialism and imperialism were discredited and the African continent was moving irresistibly towards freedom. Colonialism was coming to an end and the former colonies were moving towards liberation, but in South Africa, things weren't reversed. In fact, under the apartheid government, conditions for the native people were getting worse. Outside of South Africa, freedom had come to the Gold Coast, which became the new state of Ghana. Patrice Lumumba and his Congolese National Movement were (against a reluctant and double-dealing Belgium) pulling his country, the Congo, towards freedom and a date with destiny. To complement that was taking place in the rest of Africa, the Pan Africanist Congress (PAC) of Azania was born in 1959.

With the UTTGC dissolved and the TTA installed in its place, there were no visible changes yet in the day-to-day lives of the people. The Nationalist government was proceeding headlong with its apartheid measures, and sporadic unrest was breaking out as a result of the implementation of this irksome policy. Nonetheless, we were not prepared for the serious and widespread peasant revolt that engulfed the country in 1960. When people realised that the important duty of the tribal authorities was to serve the government as a fifth column, they spurned them. In that environment, people's lives were in great jeopardy.

By and large, in Thembuland itself and the rest of Transkei, the government was able to contain the simmering revolt. It was in Mpondoland that we were to see the full intensity of the uprising which, for some time, appeared to have gone out of control. It started flickeringly in the Mbizana district, but soon showed signs of gaining strength and gathering momentum. At people's meetings, the tribal authorities were denounced. The government did not heed the call to disband them. The members of these tribal authorities had been the people's leaders, but the people now rejected them. The authorities, however, did not accept the people's rejection and obstinately chose to defy the people.

The situation soon reached boiling point, in Mbizana, the Sikelweni Tribal Authority members were manhandled and the chairman chastised publicly. The tribal authority members were disgusted at what they called "mob violence" and were determined not to submit to the mob. The enraged crowd torched and razed their homesteads to the ground. The revolt spilled over to adjacent Flagstaff and soon engulfed the whole of Eastern Mpondoland. Then came the alarming report that a senior Mpondo chief, Vukayibambe Sigcau, had met a violent death, having been attacked and killed at his home and Great Place at Ntlenzi. Chief Vukayibambe was a tough, no-nonsense leader. He was also Paramount Botha Sigcau's younger brother and strongman.

His death sent shockwaves throughout Eastern Mpondoland. The message it sent to the Paramount was unmistakable: his time was up. His followers deserted him and even his servants disappeared. He was on his own, unprotected and defenceless. He drove to Lusikisiki in panic and told the magistrate he was relinquishing the Paramountcy and fleeing to save his life. The magistrate refused to accept his resignation and assured him the government would take him to a place of safety, until peace and stability had been restored. The Mpondo Paramount was taken to a place of hiding where he spent several dreary months. Torn by fear and anxiety for his future, he looked, to those who saw him, a broken man, drained and haggard. Just five years previously, his position had looked unassailable. His mere presence had been enough to ensure the safety of Mr Leppan and his entourage and to save them from imminent death at Mantusini. Now the wheel had turned full circle and he was a fugitive with no place to hide in Mpondoland.

The insurgents fondly imagined that now that Chief Botha, the White government's nominee, had been forced to flee, they had restored the *status ante quo*. However, this was 1960 and the clock could not be turned back that easily. Nonetheless, confident that control over their affairs had slipped out of the government's hands, they went to Nelson Sigcau. It was government interference that had given the Paramountcy to Botha instead of Nelson, whom amaMpondo believed was the rightful heir. Excitedly, they told Nelson, "We have come to escort you to Qawukeni to assume your rightful position. Botha has vacated and fled." It must have been a heart-breaking moment for Nelson.

He had fought a long, but unsuccessful legal battle against government's preference for Botha. The dispute had gone to the highest court in the land and he had lost. Now, after 21 years, people were telling him that he had won at last. He resisted the temptation to go along with the thrill of the passing moment. He told them, weighing his words carefully, that they were not out of the woods and that the White man's government had not been defeated. This was just an interlude and who knew how long it would last? If he went to Qawukeni, he would merely be giving the government an excuse to arrest him. He said he would then be made to answer for the insurrection and death of Vukayibambe and others.

It was a bitter pill for the insurgents to swallow. They wanted a triumphant march to Qawukeni, with all its significance and implications. They left dejected, sensing they had lost their trump card. Although they felt let down and accused Nelson of cowardice, looking back it is difficult to fault him. On the contrary, it is more correct to say that he showed commendable discretion and a mature assessment of the situation. The insurgents, however, saw it differently. They said they had been disappointed to find that the White man had succeeded in castrating Nelson at last.

The revolt raised the people's expectations and hopes. It called for a lot of courage, and it was revealed that that was a commodity the common people had in abundance. It also called for a readiness to sacrifice and thousands of ordinary people rose up to the challenge. In life, there are choices to be made. When there is a call to stand up and be counted, that is a crucial moment and if that opportunity is missed, consequences are usually dire. What is most important is that the people made a stand and, in going into the future, that will be a source of strength; it will always be remembered. The question, however, must still be asked: what positive results did all the courage and sacrifice yield? When a close analysis is made, what does the scorecard show? It must be conceded that, overall, the people suffered a crushing defeat and it is hurtful to find that all their success turned out to be ephemeral. When all is said and done, in the end it all came to "as you were".

Does that mean that the tremendous and selfless effort was in vain? No, definitely not. It is far better to have tried and failed than not to have tried at all. The truest test of a person's calibre, is the will and resolve to do one's best. It was a vivid demonstration that the government had come out on top when Chief Botha was able to come out of hiding, and openly and safely return and resume his position as Pondo Paramount. For the rest of his life, though, he could never forget the lesson, "Beware of the people's wrath!"

Let us now return to Mbizana district where the upheaval began. Here, one is happy to say, it was not all defeat. What's the good story to be told? At the beginning of the unrest, Mr Anderson Ganyile and other leaders of the resistance were charged, convicted and sentenced to imprisonment. They lodged an appeal and waited for almost a year for the result. When the result finally came that they had lost the appeal, the revolt in Eastern Mpondoland was already in full swing. On the day they went to hand themselves in to start serving their sentence, they were accompanied by thousands who were not sullen or morose.

The mighty throng was singing and dancing in exuberance of revolutionary fervour and a show of solidarity with their convicted leaders. It was also a defiant demonstration that the struggle continued. As a counter-blow to the spiteful and vindictive authorities, it was decided to boycott the town henceforth. No visit to the town would be allowed on any excuse or pretext. The government officials and local White traders did not take this seriously and thought it was just empty talk and wishful thinking. They were in for a big surprise, as the trial of strength had just begun.

On the very first day of the boycott, the usual hustle and bustle of traffic was missing and customers absent; even the doctor's surgeries were empty. The atmosphere was eerie and unreal. At the best of times, a boycott is always difficult to enforce and maintain. The strong spirit, unity of purpose, discipline and determination the people showed was unbelievable. There was no need to resort to violence and intimidation. It was the people's will to succeed that sustained them and enabled them to withstand all pressure to break the boycott. People remained steadfast in their commitment to show the government and traders that they could hit them where it hurt most.

The shopkeepers were surprised that the boycott was 100% effective but did not expect it to last. They were alarmed when a week ended with no sign of the boycott slackening. Into the second week their nerves had begun to fray and they were showing signs of desperation and beseeching the government to do something. Some were even suggesting that Mr Ganyile and his companions should be released as a bargaining chip. The boycott continued unshaken for two months and it was in its third month when Dr H.F. Verwoerd, the South African Prime Minister, made his historic speech to parliament in Cape Town, where he promised that Nationalists wanted peace and wanted to give Blacks something to be proud of, namely homelands.

Chapter 11

The Qhitsi revolt

The Mbizana boycott was undoubtedly one of the finest demonstrations of the awesome grandeur and strength of the people's power. The conclusion is inescapable that when Verwoerd made his unexpected and dramatic speech, the Mbizana boycott was also a powerful driving factor, but more of that, *anon.*

At the pinnacle of the Bantu Authorities setup was the TTA with its chairman, Paramount Botha. Describing members of these bodies as puppets was not far-fetched. The reading of the speech by Chief K.D. Matanzima in reply to De Wet Nel is a case in point. The contents of the speech were blatantly false and could not have come from African people outside of a lunatic asylum. Even members of the NP had complaints and demands to make to the government, their government. According to the speech, of all the people of South Africa, the Africans were the most satisfied group! They had no grievances and all they wished to do was express their thanks and gratitude!

On the question of Bantu Authorities, the government was not prepared to change course, and was not prepared to modify the policy, even for the sake of the safety of the chiefs and headmen. It was sticking to its discredited policy, but would provide home guards to the chiefs and headmen. Supporters of the government were dubbed as sell-outs. The Thembu monarch declined the offer of home guards, saying his sound relationship with his people was a sure guarantee of his safety. He also quipped that he could do with some protection *from* and not *by* the government. Chiefs like K.D. Matanzima welcomed the home guards and, in truth, needed them. They felt no embarrassment at having to depend on protection by the government, but rather took it as confirmation of their status and importance.

People were now in the unhappy period of intolerance and bitterness. As the head of Qamata Tribal Authority and then rising up the Bantustan ladder, was a K.D. Matanzima we did not know before. The man brooked no opposition, was heartless and ruthless. It is said that he desperately wanted to be loved, but all he received was respect and fear. He was respected for his intellect, strength of character and fearlessness. It must have irked him to observe the genuine love and affection the Thembu monarch, Sabata, received from all people, young and old. He missed that warmth and closeness. His demand for unquestioning loyalty was irrational. If you crossed K.D., you were bound to suffer. The stories are countless; it had almost become routine.

A good example is his quarrel with the people of Qhitsi in his home district, St Mark's. Deliwe, the Qhitsi headman, was a K.D. supporter, whilst his people were not. A frequent visitor to Qamata, he reported to his people that K.D. had decreed the area was marked for rehabilitation and that fencing of the area would start soon. The people were outraged and told Deliwe, that K.D. must be mad. They added for good measure that K.D. had better come himself to tell them that rubbish. Deliwe reported back to K.D. and, some days later he turned up at Qhitsi, accompanied by an armed force. As residents were still pondering this turn of events, they noticed the arrival of two police vans, which parked at a vantage point.

The men of Qhitsi feared an attack and fled to the hills. K.D. and his men proceeded to Deliwe's place and conferred with him before advancing on the village. They set fire to five huts allegedly belonging to the ring leaders. They also took two cattle and some goats and drove them to Qamata as booty. The policemen in the vans had watched all this happen and when darkness fell, they left. After the police had left, the local men came down from the hills and went straight to Deliwe's place. They surrounded the homestead and, when Deliwe appeared at the doorway, they mocked him. "So, you did not go to Qamata with your father, Matanzima? That's good, we are going to deal with you." They killed him mercilessly but spared his family.

Later, 54 men from Qhitsi were to appear in the Circuit Court in Butterworth on a charge of murder. After weighing the evidence, the presiding judge was evidently of the view that extenuating circumstances outweighed the aggravating features in this case. He was considering a suspended sentence but then, as a precaution, asked the state prosecutor to give the court an update of the security situation in Qhitsi. At the suggestion of the state prosecutor, the District Commissioner was called in to give the court the lowdown on security at Qhitsi. He gave the court a sombre picture. The prevailing mood was anti-government and anti-Matanzima, with the pro-government people a fearful minority. If the accused were to return now, it would be a setback for the government.

With that assessment, the fate of the Qhitsi men was sealed. The judge took the cue and his mood changed. He condemned in the strongest terms their cowardly attack on Deliwe, in his home, in front of his wife and children. He scorned them for scampering to the hills like frightened rabbits in the face of Chief Matanzima and his men. Only towards the end did he soften a little and concede there had been grave provocation. However, he added, they had not acted in the heat of the moment, but waited for darkness before sneaking out like wolves. All 54, including two septuagenarians, were sentenced to 15 years' imprisonment with hard labour.

In the neighbouring district of Glen Grey, the mood was strongly and defiantly anti-government. The government and its agents, such as Chief K.D., were engaged in a campaign of infiltration, but with moderate success. K.D.'s only significant gain was to win the support of Chief Manzezulu Mtirara of Mbinzana. The headman of Rwantsana, Sitolotolo, also went over to the government side without carrying the people with him. Calling him a sell-out, they killed him. Sitolotolo was victim of the prevailing intolerance and bitterness. The anti-government forces were engaged in a bitter struggle to prevent the spread of the pro-government virus in the district and in the process exceeded the bounds of moderation.

Forty men from Rwantsana faced a charge of murder in the Circuit Court at Queenstown. Mr Mpitizeli Zoya, his brother Khatyana Zoya, as well as a third man, their cousin, were found guilty of murder and sentenced to death. The rest were found not guilty and discharged. After the verdict and the sentence had been pronounced, outside the court, Matanzima's praise singer broke into a panegyric. It was a bizarre and obscene spectacle. This was symptomatic of the inhumane behaviour and feeling that had infected our society, a society that seemed not to know the difference between right and wrong or between good and evil.

Chapter 12

African nationalism and apartheid collide

In order to appreciate fully the root causes of this uncontrollable anger, we must also look at the actions of the government and its officials and agents. People's lives were destroyed or ruined as government enforced its policy and dealt harshly with all opposition. It is no exaggeration to say it was a matter of life and death. The ruthlessness of the government, plus the brutal nature of the system itself, put peoples' nerves on edge. The government did not tolerate even the criticism of its policy. It had sacked hundreds of teachers who openly opposed its Bantu Education policy. Under the leadership of the CATA, teachers had been at the forefront of the liberatory struggle.

The government was using education as a tool in its campaign to entrench White supremacy and Black subordination. These teachers were fighting for true and unadulterated education in their struggle for full citizenship for all. The whole executive of CATA had been dismissed and the teachers' organisation severely crippled. With CATA out of the way, the forces opposed to the government were severely weakened. The government was now able to proceed faster and more easily in advancing its programme. Without enlightened leadership, people are inclined to act impulsively and unwisely in their frustration. Strict adherence to a principled struggle is essential to avoid the danger of adventurism and opportunism.

The Belgian Congo was heading for independence and there was growing concern among the masses that South Africa was not marching in step with the events in the rest of Africa. It was at this time that the PAC appeared on the scene and found a warm and fervent response from the African masses. The reason for this is simple. The PAC was a call for an African voice and an African agenda, driven by Africans themselves. It was a repudiation of the spurious claim that South Africa was a White man's country. It boldly proclaimed: "Afrika, izwe lethu!!" – "Africa, land of our birth." This call was to resonate throughout the sub-continent, inspiring envy and fear from White supremacists.

A clear and concise statement, forthright and unapologetic, it was the simple truth. Because it was also a rallying call against domination and subjugation, it was seen by privileged White South Africans as treason and an abomination. PAC zealots called themselves "out-and-out Africans", that is, "AmaAfrika Poqo". Poqo became a terrifying word, enough to cause a running stomach for the faint-hearted. African youth were holding their heads high. The PAC was not addressing "Baas Nel" and had no "Baas".

In response to the PAC's very first campaign, a non-violent campaign, the government was heavy-handed where innocent blood was shed at Langa Township in Cape Town and in the Sharpeville massacre in the Vaal on 21 March 1960.[55] Human relations were now poisoned and the government was not in a conciliatory mood. It was not considering any placatory moves and, instead, showed a determination to crush any revolt or challenge to its domination. As government officials were to say, "Peace and order will be maintained at all costs," and, "Any violence, incitement to violence, or disturbance of the peace, will be severely dealt with." In line with this show of strength, political organisations were banned and the country placed under a state of emergency.

At the same time, Belgium had reneged on its intention to grant the Congo full independence and had attacked the new country because the Lumumba government refused to accept neo-colonialist status. When the South African government was busy suppressing the peasant revolt, amaMpondo called what was taking place "the Congo". The Verwoerd government clamped down on civil liberties, virtually placing the country under martial law. It was against this background that Dr H.F. Verwoerd dramatically announced his Bantu homelands proposals. He wanted to be seen to be charting a way forward that would extricate the country from the morass in which it had become stuck. One thing he was not prepared to do, however, was to backtrack on apartheid.

There is an aphorism that reads, "When things go wrong, a wise man knows the first suspect should be himself." Of course, we could never expect *that* from the advocates of apartheid. One of the most revolting aspects of apartheid advocates was their unctuous rectitude. It was as if they were proclaiming the gospel and not merely expressing a point of view. With apartheid, there never was room for debate and the government never wavered or decided to rethink their ideas. They had a ready-made answer to explain away the revulsion against apartheid and the unrest that was shaking the whole country. For the Nationalists, it was communism and communist-inspired malcontents and terrorists who were behind it all.

---

55   A number of people were killed by police at Langa Township and 69 people at Sharpeville. By 9 April, the death toll had risen to 83 non-White civilians and three non-White police officers. Online: www.sahistory.org.za [Accessed 9 January 2019].

Dr H.F. Verwoerd took South Africa by surprise with his announcement: "In the fulfilment of the government's policy of giving to each his own, the government wanted to ensure a peaceful and prosperous future for all South Africa's people, White and Black." Towards this end, he was announcing "the preparedness and readiness of the government to hand over land for the establishment of homelands for South Africa's Black nations". That was the only way of peaceful co-existence. Even as he spoke, the situation on the ground was worsening. Chiefs and headmen on whom the government relied had lost their power and authority and now needed government protection themselves. The government was forced to provide home guards for their safety.

For the time being, the White communities in towns and villages, as well as the isolated traders in rural areas were safe. However, the government had to think ahead and plan accordingly. With the Mbizana boycott in mind, the government had to be prepared for any eventuality. If things were to change and these White communities threatened, how would the government ensure their safety and protection?

It was against this background that Dr H.F. Verwoerd outlined his plans for Bantu homelands. His motivation was not generosity or altruism, but cool, cold-blooded calculation and concern for the safety of White lives. In the reserves, he proposed the take-over of all trading stations in the rural areas by the Bantu Development Corporation, which would, in due course, hand them over to suitable Bantu owners. In the towns and villages, the government would start a zoning system to facilitate a gradual and smooth Bantu take-over. In the Transkei, the government was already far ahead in its scheme of transforming the TTA to a fully-fledged Legislative Assembly.

By and large, the White rural traders did not welcome their proposed "eviction" and the government had to use all its powers of persuasion plus a promise of handsome pay-outs. Those in the towns and villages were stonewalling, saying in the main that any disruption in the schooling of their children was unwelcome. The government had to do a lot of pleading and cajoling. The exception was Mbizana, where all traders to a man were keen and anxious to sell, unlike their brethren elsewhere who were busy arguing and haggling. In Mbizana, the boycott had taught them a lesson they would not forget and they did not wish for an encore.

In the town of Butterworth, when the zoning committee came and asked the local Whites what portion of the town they wanted to be zoned Black, they said none. The Butterworth Municipality and the Transkei Chamber of Commerce said Butterworth should remain White. They said traders in the rural areas and the surrounding districts of Centane and Nqamakwe were selling and coming to Butterworth. Their children attended school in Butterworth, where there was a high school. When urged by the commission to point out some part, they could only point to somewhere on the commonage.

What was interesting was a proposal presented by some African gentlemen – C.W. Monakali, .I.G.Z. Mama and J.Q. Mnyani (or H.H. Masebe) – who were all self-appointed and not representing any body or group. They asked for a small strip on the eastern edge of town next to the railway-line. In their own words, "You will notice that we did not open our mouths too wide. We have left the lion's share of both business and residential areas to our White friends. We trust that you will grant us our modest request."

Listening to this grovelling, this author, who was present, experienced annoyance and disgust and asked also to be heard. Before allowing him to speak, the Chairman, who had come from Pretoria, enquired if he was present when the other Black gentlemen had made their representation. After he had replied in the affirmative, he was asked if there was anything he wished to add. Just as the poor fellow was about to speak, the Chairman added, "Do you disagree with anything those gentlemen said?" The fellow answered, "They said they had given the lion's share to their White friends. This is not a jungle where there are lions, hyenas and jackals." The Chairman cut him short, "No more of that. Don't come here to criticise other people. Be respectful. Now what do you want to tell us? Come near the table and speak up clearly so we can hear you."

The young fellow moved up and spoke as follows, "At present, only two properties are owned by Africans, the two boarding houses in this town. I can give you the names of 70 people working here with no houses and they want property to buy. At the Regional Office of Education, there are six inspectors. At the Magistrate's office, there are five senior clerks. There is a doctor and an attorney." He went on and when summing up, he observed, "I ask for land to be made available now. It is not realistic to wait till some White owner decides he wants to sell."

The chairman remarked, "You have not told us what portion you ask to be zoned Black?" The young fellow replied, "I ask that all restrictions be removed to enable Africans to buy and settle anywhere in Butterworth." The chairman interjected, "You want the whole town to be zoned Black?" The young fellow insisted, "That is not my language. I do not speak colour."

The chairman thanked the speakers for their input and the fine spirit in which the matter was handled. He noted that there was only one jarring note that had come at the end. It was not in consonance with the cordial relations that existed between races here. So, with the chairman, it translated to cordial relations if Whites had the lion's share. In any event, what the young fellow had said had goaded them to do something and pretty soon. Within a year, plots were made available in what had previously been the Coloured Township.

After another year, zoning was done and an area more or less along the lines requested by the "respectful Blacks" was zoned Black and then opened for Black occupation.

Chapter 13

The Bantustan imbroglio

Cofimvaba district was given to Chief K.D. Matanzima and the government was keen to make the area a showpiece to woo and entice doubters and confound critics and sceptics. The government also wished to soften the blow for dissidents in the district. The irrigation scheme introduced in Qamata and Sidutyini was not just a cosmetic thing, but something genuine that raised the level of farming. It raised the stature of K.D. himself as somebody who was listened to by the government and who could – and did – get things done.

In the rest of Thembuland, the government used lies and blackmail to deny people the infrastructure and amenities they asked for. Their standard reply when people wanted amenities such as dams or windmills and the like, was the lame excuse that all those things fell under the Bantu Authorities, which their selfish and headstrong sovereign rejected. In the Ngcobo district, the senior Thembu Chief was Zwelihle Mtirara of Quluqu. He was the grandson of Busobengwe, son and heir of Silimela, who was the son of Ngangelizwe in a junior house. Chief Zwelihle had just taken over the chieftainship from his uncle, Hlathikhulu, who had been regent for some years. He had a pleasant disposition, was highly intelligent and progressive in outlook. He was very close to his cousin, the Paramount Sabata, and the two complemented each other well. Onlookers saw a bright future for the Thembu nation with these two working together when, seemingly out of the blue, the unexpected happened.

It was reported that Chief Zwelihle had died in an attack in his home, the Great Place at Quluqu. It was as if a thunderbolt had come out of clear sky and struck somebody dead. We could not make any sense of this bizarre affair. To the best of our knowledge and belief, Chief Zwelihle had no known enemies and was a likeable individual. We could not fathom the whys and wherefores of this brutal murder. We could not puzzle out the riddle as to who stood to gain from the seemingly senseless killing. In spite of the disturbed state of affairs in Thembuland, he had not made enemies and was on the correct side of the fence. To say we were nonplussed is to put it mildly. Nobody had been arrested and, from all reports, the police had no clues. This gruesome killing had all the indications that it was the work of professionals.

The only professional killers we knew in Transkei were members of the South African Army and the Police Special Services. We could not imagine any reason why they would target the chief and could find no good reason to suspect them. On the other hand, it was not easy to accept that this professional work was a local Thembu job. It was not that abaThembu could not and did not kill each other. However, when killings occurred, they were the result of disputes and quarrels which were well known and the traces and other incriminating evidence would often be easy to find. Even now, 50 years later, we are still none the wiser as to who the culprits were. Various theories were bandied about, but we were never able to get to the bottom of the matter.

One theory which, though untested, did sound fairly plausible was that this was an internal Quluqu affair with no outsider involved. According to this theory, the government had tried unsuccessfully to persuade the Qwathi and Chief Sakhela Dalasile to do a Matanzima at Ngcobo. Having failed to woo the Qwathi, the government turned their attention to Chief Zwelihle who had the added advantage that he was high in the Thembu hierarchy. The government was after a big quarry.

According to this theory, the government officials approached Chief Zwelihle and made their proposals. The chief and some councillors were considering these blandishments with no decision reached. They had failed to inform the Paramount of the matter and were secretive about the negotiations. By so doing, Chief Zwelihle had compromised himself already and his negotiations were treasonable. Fearing the worst, some councillors decided to nip the conspiracy in the bud and not give treason any chance to blossom at Quluqu. The big government attendance at the funeral lends some credence to the story and, in fact, suggests that maybe some agreement had been reached.

From the magistrate's fine speech, one was not able to glean any pointers. It was the attendance and oration of Hans Abraham, the Commissioner-General, that was rather revealing. A Commissioner-General was a queer post, like a cross between a *Gauleiter* (a German governor over a conquered people) and a Consul. Hans Abraham, occupying a post that required tact and diplomacy, was blunt and crude – an undiplomatic diplomat! But then, is diplomacy necessary, were good manners a prerequisite when dealing with natives? His *"Groot Baas"* stance was an unnecessary and stupid provocation.

From his speech it was clear he had not come to express any condolences to the Thembu nation, the royal house or the Silimela family. He was there to make a political diatribe. Thus, he went into a tirade berating anarchists, communists and terrorists and all those evil-minded people who were poisoning good relations between Blacks and Whites. He castigated those individuals who were spreading false doctrines and misleading the Bantu and teaching them to hate and despise their customs and institutions. Evil things were happening that were shocking and unheard of.

He knew the people whose teachings had resulted in gruesome murders like this one, and he wanted to name and shame them. The culprit was Patrick Duncan and he bore full responsibility for this shedding of innocent blood. To put the blame for the death of Chief Zwelihle squarely upon Patrick Duncan seemed rather far-fetched and disingenuous. Duncan was the son of the last governor-general. His crime seemed to be that he was the leader of the Liberal Party in South Africa and liked to go to the Transkei, to try and sway people against Bantustans, saying that was dividing South Africa.

It was always strange when one listened to people like Hans Abraham speaking; one felt as if one had met the lunatic fringe. With all this stuff and nonsense, the man took himself seriously. This reminded one of "a tale told by an idiot, full of sound and fury, but signifying nothing".

Chapter 14

The Mthentu dispute

Contempt for people's feelings was one of the worst wrongs committed by colonialism/imperialism. The story of Mthentu in the Mthatha District, and the frustration of its residents under the obstinate, headstrong and uncaring government officials, is one of the most sickening accounts of life under colonialist rule.

As the struggle against Bantu Authorities intensified, many brutal murders were committed on both sides of the divide. One of the most horrific was the killing of the tough and fearless Dadeni Grwababa, headman of the Mthentu Administrative Area, in 1960.

The rightful headman, Sithethi Veliso, fell foul of the law and was removed from his position after conviction for unlawfully receiving money from applicants for land. He was sentenced to six months' imprisonment, and his cousin, Dadeni Grwababa, was then appointed headman. By all accounts, Dadeni was a tough customer who ruled Mthentu with an iron hand and brooked no nonsense.

Sithethi duly served his term of imprisonment and returned to civilian life. Chafing under Dadeni's strict and rigid control, people yearned for the benign rule of the placid Sithethi. Their attempts to have Sithethi forgiven and reinstated as headman did not succeed and they handed the case to an attorney. Their contention was that Sithethi's transgression should be condoned as he had erred, but once and had paid for his sin. People respected and trusted him as head of the senior house of the amaZizi at Mthentu, the Menziwa family.

The South African government agreed to put the matter to a vote for the people to decide. Sithethi's supporters were overjoyed and they won the vote comfortably. Evidently, the government did not expect this outcome and now stalled and prevaricated. Finally, the government's response was that: No good cause had been shown why a reliable and hardworking headman like Dadeni should be removed from his post.

It is said the chief magistrate, J.J. Yates, confided to the Mthentu people's attorney that the government found itself in a predicament in Dadeni's case. Ordinarily, the government had no difficulty in obliging and appointing the candidate favoured by the people. That usually works best for everybody concerned. But the government found Dadeni to be someone special. In Mthatha district, he had distinguished himself in that:

1. The Mthentu Admin Area had always been regarded as one of the most difficult to manage. The court/ibandla was strong and fiercely independent and always had the headman firmly under control. Dadeni had proved to be more than their (ibandla) match and had turned the tables against them. He had his court firmly under his grip.

2. In the periodic court at Bhityi, for the area bordering the Mbhashe River, Mthentu provided most of the cases. Law breakers and transgressors were brought to justice and there was no impunity.

3. All African male adults at the time were liable to pay an annual poll tax in the amount of R2,00. Dadeni was conscientious and zealous in urging and goading taxpayers to pay. There were no tax defaulters at Mthentu and Dadeni received a bonus yearly from the government. The government was loath to abandon its good and faithful servant.

That was in 1949. Years rolled by and, moving forward to 1960, it was the time of the Peasant Revolt in Transkei (spasmodic in Thembuland, sustained in Mpondoland. First, the Mthentu people had tried to use the Bantu Authorities Act as their instrument to remove Dadeni. They then took their complaint to the Dalindyebo Regional Authority, which upheld Sithethi Veliso's claim. The final word, however, had to come from the government in Pretoria, which proved intransigent and contended that Dadeni deserved a promotion and not relegation and refused to budge.

In 1960, the people were no longer in a supplicatory mood and told Dadeni the time had come for him to choose who to obey – the people or the government. Next, they told him if he wished to live in peace, he should give up the headmanship, otherwise he was endangering his own life. Dadeni was adamant he would not vacate his position, come what may. The patience of Mthentu residents had been stretched to the limit. They felt they had no option after persuasion had failed, except to take drastic action. They killed him in a merciless manner – surrounded his home, set it alight, and when he tried to escape, they butchered him.

The government was unforgiving and declared that murderers and criminals at Mthentu had challenged the government to a test of wills, but they would be the losers in that contest. Their candidate, Sithethi Veliso, had forfeited any claim to the headmanship. To show that the government was unyielding, it declared that Dadeni's heir would be the headman. This was also meant as a tribute to Dadeni's fidelity and courage in the service of the government.

Dadeni became another in the long list of unwitting stooges who put their lives on the line and sacrificed their all at the altar of White supremacy. Dadeni was a courageous man with a strong will who was not afraid to go against the wishes of the community in the service of an unpopular cause. Without doubt, he could have lived and died better.

The government's stubborn refusal to accede to popular demand ensured that the Mthentu dispute would never come to an end, but would go on and on and on. By the same token, the house of Grwababa – imposed on an unwilling citizenry – would never find legitimacy and acceptance as headmen.

There is a twist to this saga: Dadeni himself was known to accept money from applicants for land, but the government turned a blind eye to that. In the government's view, Dadeni put the government's interests above all else. The government's bowl was full to overflowing. What if he took some pickings for himself, was that such a big deal?

Chapter 15

AbaThembu are co-opted

The death of Chief Zwelihle left a void and was a great loss to the Thembu Royal House, which was seriously lacking in men of strong character and great intellect. In fact, the sovereign stood head and shoulders above a motley collection of mediocre individuals who constituted the house of Mtirara at the time. The Joyis of Mputi were the exception. They showed independence of mind and a determination to resist the government-sponsored carving up of Thembuland, the diminution of the status of the sovereign and the nurturing and build-up of K.D. Matanzima.

In 1958, the Minister of Bantu Administration and Development, De Wet Nel, had installed the Mpondo Paramount Botha Sigcau as Chairman of the TTA. The peasant revolt of 1960 had left the Mpondo Paramount severely strained and exhausted both physically and emotionally. It was more than enough for him to have been restored to his shaky seat at Qawukeni. He just hoped and wished to be allowed to live a quiet and peaceful life. Public occasions and all the ceremonials had become onerous and a drudgery. Even TTA sittings were unwelcome and tedious experiences. It was thus inevitable and in fact expected, when the ambitious and self-seeking Chief K.D. Matanzima became Chairman in 1963. Chief K.D. was not tired and weary, but fresh and raring to go. He was looking to the future with great expectations and all things seemed to be going his way.

Chief K.D. was not being pushed or coerced. He had become a true convert and had given himself over body and soul to the service of apartheid. While abaThembu saw a dark cloud looming ominously, spoiling the present and imperiling the future, K.D. was viewing a bright horizon and a bright future was beckoning. He was confident and assured and had no qualms or misgivings.

The Thembu sovereign received instructions from the government requesting him to officiate and install Chief K.D. Matanzima as chief over the Xhalanga district. In its dealing with the government, the Thembu Great House had always adopted a principled stand. The correct and principled position on this request for the sovereign to go and officiate in this irregular installation should have been a blunt refusal. The sovereign should have flatly refused to rubber-stamp a wrong and crooked government decision. Further, the sovereign should have stated unequivocally that the district of Xhalanga was and remains an integral part of Thembuland and would not be part of any spurious and irregular creation, the fictitious so-called "Western Thembuland".

Those councillors who adopted this stand encountered strong opposition. There was another group of councillors who criticised the confrontational stand. They said this negative approach had proved to be counter-productive. This refusal to work with the government had not prevented the government from doing what it wanted. In their view, the time had come to change tactics. The government no longer took seriously anything the Thembu said. It was said they were referred to in government circles as "the No's" because they said no to everything. "Let us surprise them and say yes this time," was the majority's view. "We will lose nothing thereby. Instead, who knows, we might start a new era of co-operation with both Matanzima and the government." Misled and accompanied by these councillors, the Thembu sovereign went to Cala for Chief K.D. Matanzima's installation.

The crowd at Cala was unruly and unmanageable and the installation was performed to the accompaniment of loud booing and catcalls. Cala residents were determined to show their rejection of the imposition of K.D. as their unwanted chief. The booing and catcalls reached a crescendo as the sovereign performed the ceremony with these curt and telling words, "I have been instructed to install you and I do so." Even at the worst of times, the true Sabata always managed to come out.

Several men were arrested for disorderly conduct and duly charged in the Cala magistrate's court. True to its time-old practice of using the Chief against his own people, the government made Sabata the complainant. The accused were charged with showing the sovereign contempt and disrespect. All the accused were found not guilty and discharged. In his evidence, Sabata said the people did not show him contempt or disrespect. On the contrary, they showed they held him in high esteem. They were objecting to his forced participation in a wrongful government exercise. The person they showed contempt and disrespect for was K.D. and he should be the complainant. The men left the court smiling and outside saluted their sovereign, "Ah! Jonguhlanga!"

In pursuit of their agenda, the apartheid government was brazen and showed utter disregard for people's feelings and susceptibilities. It was not even a stance of "take it or leave it"; it was simply, take it and be damned. It is useful to find the reason behind this madness, for there was good reason for their apparent lunacy.

The government's obsession with creating a spurious Paramountcy for Chief K.D. Matanzima was not driven by any lunatic delusion. It was a cool, cold-blooded calculation. The Bantustan edifice was built on chieftainship and as their chosen pilot for the scheme, Chief K.D. Matanzima, had to be provided with the appropriate equipage and paraphernalia for the position. Among the leaders was also the Xhosa monarch, Zwelidumile, coming from a long line of illustrious sovereigns. There was also the Mpondo Paramount – albeit the incumbent was a government appointee. Most importantly, the leadership included the Thembu monarch, Sabata, who was recalcitrant, with all his charisma and popular acclaim.

Something had to be done to provide their choice of Bantustan head with the wherewithal, to put him on a par with these august personages. It would not do to pick a bedraggled nincompoop to do the job. A pukka traditional leader had to be found and groomed to become the first among equals and not a first among his superiors. Only then can one appreciate and understand the rationale behind these apparently stupid and threadbare machinations the government undertook in its endeavour to create a Paramountcy for Chief K.D. Matanzima.

If one cannot find the authentic, it makes sense to create it. With Chief K.D. Matanzima, the government chose well. He was good at playing the part and it seems he himself came to believe that he was a genuine Paramount and not an apartheid creation. That pretence continues. Now that traditional leaders (to use the current phrase) had been debased by government infiltration and manipulation, it was not difficult for Chief K.D. Matanzima to feel at ease in their midst and deem himself to be their equal. That was in the beginning. In the end, as leader of the Transkei National Independence Party and Bantustan premier, he called the shots. He now regarded himself as their superior, and they were his underlings, but of this, *anon*. Thembuland and Thembuland alone was still holding fast in its determination and resolve to reject Bantu Authorities.

Unexpectedly and abruptly, Thembuland took a decision to join the Bantustan bandwagon. This decision was precipitated by a shocking and disturbing proposal from the Ngcobo district, of all places. In the fight against government seduction and infiltration, Ngcobo had been a tower of strength. Ngcobo had rejected with contempt all blandishments the government offered. To everybody's surprise and consternation, Ngcobo spokesmen said they had done a reappraisal and were recommending a change of strategy.

They emphasised that they were not abandoning the fight against the government's nefarious policies. They said the people were dealing with an unscrupulous and cynical government which showed no respect for Thembuland's territorial integrity.

Thembuland had been dismembered and lost three districts already and government intrigue had not ceased. Before another district was lost, the three remaining districts, Mthatha, Mqanduli and Ngcobo should *en bloc* accept Bantu Authorities and form the Dalindyebo Regional Authority. Having done that, the Dalindyebo region should join the TTA. By so doing, the Thembu would not be collaborating, but would continue the fight from within.

Of course, this was nothing, but a sellout position and abaThembu themselves knew it. Instead of telling Engcobo representatives straight, they implored them not to stray. In the end, it was not principle that prevailed, but expediency. It appeared the overriding consideration was to avoid a split. To avoid a breakaway by Engcobo, the meeting decided to accept the Engcobo proposal. With downcast eyes and heavy hearts, abaThembu abandoned a policy that had enabled them to carry their heads high through all vicissitudes. Now there was mutual suspicion and recrimination.

The split everyone feared could not be avoided. Those who felt strongly about this collaboration realised that they were no longer the majority. They realised that the vote to go to Cala for Chief K.D. Matanzima's installation was no fluke. They had ruled the roost for 40 years, but now others had taken over. It was those who promised to fight from within who took the Thembu Paramount to the TTA. They were to learn soon that the dice was loaded against them and only the government agenda was carried in that body.

With Thembuland finally, though reluctantly, in the bag, the government was able to proceed to the next step towards self-government: the dissolution of the TTA and the introduction of a Transkei Legislative Assembly. The TTA had 80 members, consisting of two elected members from each of the 26 districts of the Transkei. The government also appointed one member from each district. The Paramount Chief of Gcalekaland, the Paramount of Thembuland, as well as the Mpondo Paramount, were ex officio members. This form of representation had been inherited from the old United Transkeian Territories General Council.

The government had decided on a Transkei Legislative Assembly of 100 members. 40 would be elected by popular vote while 60 would come from the tribal authorities. According to the government's perverted sense of fair play, the matter would not be left to the people to decide. By giving the traditional leaders a big majority, the government averred the body would be a true representation of Bantu structures and the Bantu way of life. A voters' roll was also being compiled on a universal adult suffrage basis.

Family life

The young Mda

Wedding photo, June 1954. *From left to right*: Mlizeni Mda (twin sister to Nobambo), Albert Mda, Thembisa Mda (twin sister to Thembeka Mda), Mac Zulu Mda, Ms Mnengisa, Dube Mzimba, Nomachibi Ntshanga-Ngewu, Mndayi Mzimba, Mda, Dorothy Zanyiwe nèe Ntshanga, Phakama Nxiweni, Lumkile Makubalo, Nobambo Mda (Mrs Xorile) (twin to Mlizeni Mda), Monica Mda (Mrs Kobus), Mathombela Mda, Thembeka Mda (twin to Thembisa Mda), Sastri Mda and Zantsi Mzimba

On the left: Mda and Dorothy Zanyiwe nèe Ntshanga

On the right: Mda and his younger brother Sastri in Cape Town

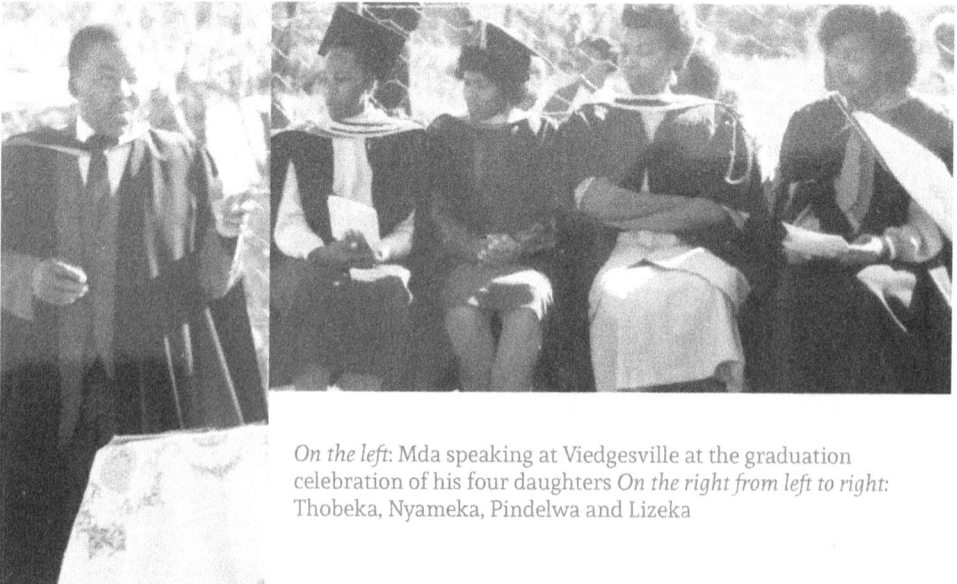

On the left: Mda speaking at Viedgesville at the graduation celebration of his four daughters *On the right from left to right*: Thobeka, Nyameka, Pindelwa and Lizeka

Christmas Day, Hurlington, Johannesburg, 2008. *In the back from left to right:* grandson Avukile Mabombo, son Zulu Mda, daughter Nyameka Mda, Mda, daughters Lizeka Mda, Pindewa Mda and grandson Tinyiko T. Mda *In the front from left to right:* Sheila Thoka (relative), granddaughter Nwabisa NwiseWise, daughter Thembeka Mda, grandsons Lesedi Alexander, Luyanda Alexander and daughter Thobeka

December 2011 at the occasion of Sastri's 80th birthday celebration with his remaining siblings then. *At the back from left to right:* Kolisa Mda, Sastri Mda, Mda, Dumisa Mda. *In the front from left to right:* Thembeka Mda, Nobambo Mda-Xorile, Pumeza Mda. (Currently Kolisa, Sastri, Mda Mda and Thembeka Mda remain.)

Sisters celebrate Thobeka's 60th birthday in 2015. *From left to right*: Pindelwa, Thembeka, Thobeka, Nyameka, Lizeka

Christmas time at Viedgesville, 2016. *In the back from left to right*: Daughters Lizeka and Nyameka, grandson Avukile, son Zulu, granddaughter Sixolile and daughter Pindelwa *Seated from left to right*: Sister Thembeka, Mda, daughter Thobeka

Political life

Brother and comrade, Sastri Mda

Dr Marina V.N. Xaba-Mokoena with Mda

Conversations Across Generations, University of Fort Hare, 29th August 2007.
In the back fom left to right: Sastri Mda, M.P. Giyose, Mda, Cornelius Thomas (organiser),
Allan Zinn (facilitator). *In the front from left to right*: Dennis Brutus, Livie Mqotsi and R.S. Canca
Photographer: Marcus Thomas

Former New Unity Movement Presidents, Richard Dudley, Reggie Feldman with Life Member Mda
in Mthatha

East London gathering, 26th January 2008. *In the back from left to right*: John Bennett, Mark Fredericks, Allan Zinn, Hammy Peterson, Stella Letanka, Joe Slingers
In the front from left to right: Basil Brown, Livie Mqotsi, M.P. Giyose, Iris Mqotsi, Mda, Aubrey Kali, Ross Sogoni

Mda and Phyllis Jordan (nèe Ntantala)

Mda speaking May 2009, in front is Felicity Titus and Mike de Leeuw and at the back is Holford Nyikane and Mda

From left to right: Mda, Dr Mvuyo Tom, Livie Mqotsi and Yolisa Soul. Handover of Mqotsi Archives to UFH

From left to the right in the back: Mervyn Blaauw, Mda and Garth van Heerden
From left to right in the front: M.P. Giyose and Goba Ndlovu

From left to right: Mda, Mickey Titus and Norman Abrahams

Mda with June Udemans from Port Elizabeth

Mda's lifelong comrade Zantsi Mzimba

Chapter 16

Every traditional leader has a price

In 1858, having been weakened by Nongqawuse, amaXhosa had been evicted and driven out of Butterworth, Nqamakwe and Tsomo. In 1865, the three districts had been given to amaMfengu and called Fingoland (Mfenguland). The territory was under the control of magistrates and there were no chiefs. Now the government decided to turn the clock back and install chiefs. It was announced that Mfengu royal families had been traced in the Tsomo district. One from the Hlubi, with the surname of Zulu, was brought to Ndabakazi and made Butterworth chief. Another, with the surname Ngcongolo, was installed as Nqamakwe chief, while one Nkwenkwezi was made chief at Tsomo. The Bantu Authorities were still continuing past divisive policies. The sane thing to do was simple and straight forward, that is, return the land to the authority of the Xhosa sovereign.

The government evidently was unaware that the ordinary people were tired of these artificial divisions. People were sick and tired of being told they were government's people, "good and loyal Fingo". They saw themselves as one with the rest of the oppressed African community. In fact, a move was already afoot to break free from government's agenda. They were cutting the umbilical cord joining them to the government. When campaigning for the Transkei Legislative Assembly started, they showed their true colours. They were asserting their inalienable right to decision-making on matters affecting their lives. It was a clear statement, they were no longer tied to the government's apron strings. The movement chose four candidates to uphold their banner and called them The Big Four. They were: Mr O. Mpondo, Dr H.P. Bala, Mr Campbell Mnyila and Mr S.M. Zokwe for the three districts, Butterworth, Nqamakwe and Tsomo, the Mfengu region. The area had always been represented by government loyalists who thought it was business as usual.

Mr J.J. Henning, the Butterworth magistrate, had told at a public meeting that this was a new era for the African people. This was an opportunity for them to elect their own representatives without any interference from the government. Henning was as true as his word. He adhered strictly to that promise. He did not use his position, authority or government resources to influence the vote. The voting was open, free and fair and the pro-government candidates received a severe drubbing. What a surprise! Mfenguland of all places, endorsing an anti-government ticket and making a clean sweep!

Shocked at this unexpected result and fearing the government programme would be derailed, Hans Abraham, the Commissioner-General, was furious. He railed at Henning, accusing him of grave dereliction of duty. With all government resources at his disposal, and his influential position, he had done nothing and just folded his arms and sat on his backside. He did not raise a finger to assist pro-government candidates and had given the anti-government agitators a free hand. He was the culprit. In Hans Abraham's eyes, Henning had sabotaged government plans. For voting in the Big Four, the common people would be made to suffer.

The vote had been touted as open, free and fair for the African electorate in Transkei. Everywhere, the pattern was the same; pro-government candidates were getting a walloping. Now that the heartland of Gcalekaland had been excised and formed into Mfenguland, the rump of Gcalekaland were the districts of Centane, Willowvale, Elliotdale and Idutywa. Even there, the anti-government candidates had a landslide victory and one Mr Joel Busakwe was credited with this result.

Of course, no single individual could achieve such a feat. This is not to deny his tremendous influence and organising power. He had been working in East London for years and had risen in the ranks of the labour movement and the Industrial and Commercial Union (ICU), founded by Clements Kadalie. He was also prominent in sporting circles and had been president of the Bushbucks Rugby Club, president of the Gompo Rugby Union and, finally, president of the Border Rugby Union. Reluctantly, and only after much and persistent persuasion, he had agreed to return to his home at Ngxutyana in Willowvale after his father's death, to take up the headmanship.

Well-informed and broadminded, he was held in high regard as the chief councillor to Chief Thabathile, son of Chief Xhelinkunzi Sigcau. Together with Chief Moses Dumalisile of the Jingqi at Shixini, they were a formidable combination. Of the 40 elected members of the Transkei Legislative Assembly, the big majority was anti-government. Interest was in the election and people had even forgotten about the 60 traditional leaders who would be getting a free passage to the Legislative Assembly. Who were these 60? What was their standing and worth? Did they have any political views?

It is often expected that traditional leaders would follow popular will. Exulting in the wave of anti-government fervour, people fondly imagined the traditional leaders would follow suit. They did not analyse the situation, nor take notice that traditional leaders were under severe pressure as never before. If people had given the membership and composition of the traditional leaders a serious look, they would have been appalled and saddened at what they saw. Starting with the big contingent from Mpondoland, the spectre was ghastly and pathetic. Yes, those were true descendants and *bona fide* members of the royal house of Faku and of other Mpondo clans. For all that veneer of legitimacy, Mpondo royalty had been irretrievably crippled during the peasant revolt. It was now too firmly embedded in government tutelage and protection to be of any real use and value to the Mpondo people themselves.

That did not apply to the miserable and pitiable Botha Sigcau alone, but to the whole caboodle. In truth, they were now government stooges. It was sickening. Countrywide, in a sinister move, the government had now recognised a host of tribal chiefs who had been ignored and regarded as non-entities for years. Suddenly they were receiving stipends and held up as traditional leaders. They felt indebted to the government and were hardly likely to rock the boat or bite the hand that fed them. The government was their sponsor and benefactor. Not to mention the Mfengu traditional leaders who had been dug up from nowhere and, to their own surprise and disbelief, brought forth and ensconced as chiefs in Butterworth, Nqamakwe and Tsomo. What on earth could ever cause them to join any silly group of agitators and malcontents opposing the government? Why would they take sides with people who despised them and regarded them as a sick joke? This would be a happy hunting ground for the government.

Of course, there were traditional leaders who regarded themselves as such in the true sense of the word. They derived their power and authority from the people and were one with the people. They owed nothing to the government and could stand up to and face it. Alas, they had become few and far between, and were largely outnumbered by a big majority of cringers and obsequious government appointees. The stark reality of this truth was to come as a shock and surprise to many. In the meantime, these drones lay low, and kept their peace, hiding their true colours in silent anonymity.

Stung by the reverses the pro-government group had suffered in the elections, Chief K.D. Matanzima decided on a propaganda drive. He chose Centane as the starting point, hoping to use his blood relationship with the Xhosa to good purpose. His mother, Nogate, was a Xhosa princess and the daughter of Chief Xhoxho of Thuthurha in Centane. That made him a nephew of the Xhosa and, as such, one who would receive favoured treatment. He held a meeting at Centane expecting a good hearing, confident of Xhosa etiquette. The bruising encounter he met was evidently unexpected and upset his composure. One Qoqonga, from the Gobe tribal area, was terrier-like in his harassment and heckling, asking, "Who invited you to come here? Have you been sent by your apartheid masters to sell their cheap propaganda here? What do you take us for, stupid ignorant Reds?"

In desperation, Chief K.D. Matanzima appealed for protection and when the Chair was unable to shield him, he implored the audience at large, in the name of Xhosa courtesy, to treat him as a guest and, in his case, the added circumstance of nephew. Qoqonga would not let go and went on: "Who are you to talk of respect and courtesy? After your shabby and disgraceful treatment of your sovereign, Sabata, you want to be treated with respect?" At his wit's end, Chief K.D. Matanzima asked if there were no police to intervene and enforce order. Qoqonga was relentless and unforgiving. "This is not Qamata where you bully people. Go and tell your masters their apartheid is not wanted here. Go and do not come back."

Poor K.D. had to give up as the audience was enjoying his unequal contest with Qoqonga.

Years later, when opposition to the government had been crushed, Chief K.D. Matanzima again visited Centane and had a very successful meeting. Flushed with success, he inquired about his tormentor, Qoqonga. When told that Qoqonga had succumbed to illness and died, he retorted, "The poor wretch had brought a curse upon himself. We royalty impart either a blessing or a curse. What he did to me was inexcusable and it shortened his life." For the record, although no post mortem was conducted, the accepted cause for Qoqonga's death was tuberculosis infection. Having been employed in Cape Town where he worked in wet and cold conditions, he took ill. Whether a royal curse was part of the poor working conditions, one takes with a liberal pinch of salt.

Chapter 17

The Xhosa succession

Just at this time, the mid-1960s, the Xhosa monarch Zwelidumile passed away, throwing the Xhosa nation into a succession crisis. AmaXhosa were quite capable of handling the matter and did not need nor want government interference. Since defeat by the imperialists, there was now government surveillance, even over purely Xhosa affairs. The deceased Zwelidumile had in 1933 succeeded his elder brother Mpisekhaya who had allegedly died without male issue. In fact, his wife was pregnant when he died. Some had cautioned that any decision on succession should wait till the woman had given birth. However, wiser counsels had prevailed, insisting there was no need to wait, as the woman had not been "lobola'd" by the nation and could not give birth to an heir. Mpisekhaya's younger brother, Bhungeni, was chosen to succeed and he became King (Bhungeni) Zwelidumile. Now, with Zwelidumile's death in 1965, history had repeated itself and again the nation was faced by a predicament which called for knowledge and wisdom.

AmaXhosa have a longer experience in dealing with these crises and their wealth of wisdom is inexhaustible. Zwelidumile had been middle-aged when he died, with no son by the queen, Nozizwe. Zwelidumile had married Queen Nozizwe late in his reign and still had only one child from the queen, a girl. He had a son who was already of age from a junior wife, a commoner. The feeling was that the son, Siwowana, did not deserve promotion and should not be the heir. It was then whispered that Mpisekhaya's widow had, in fact, given birth to a son who therefore was senior in rank to Siwowana. Messengers were dispatched post haste to Mgwali, to the widow's maiden home, to see the son. The report they brought back was that they had seen the young man Mzamo, a fine replica of his father, Mpisekhaya. The cat was among the pigeons with the news.

To amaXhosa, there was no problem; the issue was simple and straightforward. Arrangements were made to fetch the young man as the hour needed him. Mzamo was welcomed with joy and relief by the members of the royal house he visited. It was the same exclamation at every visit: "nguyise ehleli!" ("He is the spitting image of his father!") The way amaXhosa saw it was that Mpisekhaya's son, born of a commoner in a junior house, was senior in status to Zwelidumile's son, born in like circumstances. To them there was no problem, the matter had resolved itself and Mzamo was the undisputed heir. Unfortunately, the matter was not left to amaXhosa to solve in their own way.

The government saw a good opportunity to intrude and take charge. The emissaries who had gone to fetch Mzamo from Mgwali were Messrs Joe Busakwe and Moses Dumalisile. They were the people who were parading Mzamo on his visits to the Xhosa royal houses. Mpisekhaya's son, Mzamo, was the favourite and preferred choice of the anti-government forces. It made sense then for the government to take up Siwowana's cause. If they succeeded – and they had a good chance of success – they could be in a powerful position with a hold on the Xhosa monarch. Thus, they decided on Siwowana as their preferred choice as the heir for the Xhosa monarchy.

Mr Gregory, the Willowvale magistrate, called members of the Gcaleka Regional Authority and raised the question of succession. The Regional Authority members tried to stall, requesting for him to wait for the mourning period to pass when they would be ready. Gregory would not be put off by any prevarication and insisted on a straight answer to a simple question, "Did the deceased monarch have any male issue?" One Xhosa spokesman tried to explain the cause of the delay, that the matter was not that simple as they were compelled to revisit the death of the former monarch, Mpisekhaya. Gregory declared that course of action to be "out of order". He then went on to explain that Zwelidumile was not a regent, but Xhosa sovereign in his own right.

That being so, any consideration of any progeny the former monarch Mpisekhaya may have had, was entirely irrelevant. The alleged son of Mpisekhaya had missed the bus. The only estate under consideration was that of the deceased Zwelidumile. Chief K.D. Matanzima and his pro-government allies were alarmed at the prospect of the future Xhosa monarch being an anti-government supporter. The widow, Nozizwe, and the Xhosa royal house were advised to agree on the placement of Siwowana as a son in Nozizwe's house. After finalising that arrangement, the matter would be referred to the Regional Authority for its endorsement. Finally, the matter would come before the magistrate for approval and transmission to the government.

The issue of Mzamo's return and his future status had not yet got off the ground when the succession was decided, signed and sealed. Siwowana was confirmed as heir and succeeded his father as King Xolilizwe. Feeling the government had acted wrongfully and irregularly, Mzamo supporters – and they were many – sought legal opinion on the prospect of testing the government's actions in court, as well as opposing the validity of (Siwowana) Xolilizwe's appointment. All advice was that Xolilizwe had a watertight case, while it was felt that Mzamo had no leg to stand on. Mzamo was banished from the Transkei, as it was held his presence was not conducive to good order and tranquility.

Chapter 18

Ciskei follows Transkei

What was happening in Transkei was being praised as an embryo of the first Bantustan state for the Xhosa ethnic unit. The serious flaw in this argument was occasioned by the historical fact that the larger portion of Xhosaland falls outside Transkei and stretches beyond the Kei River, southward to the Gamtoos River. Could one seriously talk of Xhosaland while excluding the heart of Xhosaland? All this land was stolen during the "*kaffir* wars" from 1779-1878. Starting with the unprovoked and premeditated attack by Sir John Cradock in 1811, amaXhosa were systematically deprived of their land by the British policy of ethnic cleansing. John Cradock took a big chunk of Xhosa territory, "the Zuurveld", and drove amaXhosa all the way, out until in 1812, they were pushed beyond the Fish River. The British then unilaterally proclaimed the Fish River as the boundary between the Cape Colony and the Xhosaland.

In 1819, the avaricious British plunderers gobbled up more Xhosa land and cynically pushed the boundary to the Keiskamma River. During the 19th century of shame, the insatiable appetite of the British was to wreak havoc in the subcontinent. At the end of the war of Mlanjeni [1851-1853]), Xhosaland was wiped off the face of the map and the heart of Xhosaland taken by the conqueror and, for cheek, called "British Kaffraria".

Starting with the infamous Sir Harry Smith, who occupies pride of place in the rogues' gallery of ruffians that amaXhosa had to put up with, the British were particularly mean and dastardly towards amaXhosa. Now under apartheid, Bantustan architects were promising to restore "Xhosa honour and pride". However, how honest were the protestations? The government promised to create a viable Bantu homeland called Ciskei. The existing Ciskei was an untidy collection of scraps of land, left over when Xhosa land was annexed to the Cape Colony and became European farms. The government was not seriously making any real effort to scramble up and restore land that could form a viable Ciskei.

Instead, the hypocritical government proposed to dump the urban locations of Mdantsane and Zwelitsha into the Ciskei project. The head of this embryonic Ciskei was Mr Justice Mabandla, a fine gentleman. It would be beyond the capacity of even a genius to make a success of this impossible task. With their cheap trickery, the government decided to look for someone who could persuasively masquerade as a true Xhosa patriot. Justice Mabandla was ruled out because of his Fingo entanglement. One Lennox Sebe, a senior official in the department of education, was spotted and chosen for the job.

He was said to be a "Tshawe" from the Xhosa royal clan, belonging to the Ntinde tribe. He thus appeared to have the correct credentials to enable him to be paraded as a member of the Xhosa royal house. Later, it was said a mistake had been made and was being corrected. It was now stated that Lennox Sebe was of the house of Khambashe of the Gqunukhwebe tribe. People were not impressed and believed this was all conjecture. It was no more credible than correcting a notice of birth and explaining that the baby was a boy and not a girl, as previously announced. So Lennox Sebe's royal pedigree was suspect from the start.

This put him at a disadvantage and made him the butt of jokes that he was a poor copy of even Matanzima. Driven by his apartheid masters, Lennox Sebe engaged in the impossible task of making the unworkable work. It is a puzzle why the man persevered. Was he not allowed to quit? The only towns in his drab and poverty-stricken Ciskei were the dusty and struggling villages, Peddie, Middledrift and Keiskammahoek. Those were willingly given to the Ciskei. Alice was grudgingly given after much equivocation. The government would not even think of including towns like Fort Beaufort, Seymour, King William's Town, Komga, Stutterheim, Cathcart and Queenstown, which in fact are part of Ciskei, let alone Adelaide, Bedford, Somerset East and Dordrecht.

In Transkei, practically all towns and villages had been included. The exceptions were Matatiele, Maclear, Elliot, Indwe and Kokstad. This had resulted in an exodus of businessmen, traders and artisans from labour centres such as Cape Town and Port Elizabeth, who came to the Transkei in droves. They took over the White businesses, shops and houses, thus changing the face of Transkei towns. These new arrivals swelled the numbers of Chief K.D. Matanzima's Transkei National Independence Party (TNIP) and changed it from a party of chiefs and headmen. The support base of the TNIP changed from taciturn and fearful chiefs to opportunistic, adventurist, crafty and self-seeking business people. That was the new Transkei.

To these people, Chief K.D. Matanzima was a Messiah, and they were always at his beck and call, saluting "Ah! Daliwonga!" In contrast, Lennox Sebe's Ciskei was like a poor relation, scraping to make ends meet. It was bedraggled, unlike the affluent and ostentatious Chief K.D. Matanzima's Transkei. It is true the apartheid government was a hard master, but it is also true that Lennox Sebe was ready and willing and easy to manipulate. Lennox Sebe was more to be pitied than envied and had nothing to show for the great sacrifice he had made to serve apartheid. The poor fellow had no plums to offer. Thus, there were hardly any people who believed in the correctness of what Lennox Sebe and co were doing. The majority regarded them as silly and pretentious fools.

This Bantustan concept was the brainchild of the apartheid regime. They used the Transkei as their experiment and testing ground. The agenda was theirs and the programme a product of the NP caucus. When the Nationalist government decided the time had come to tell the Transkei Legislative Assembly to vote for independence, they just gave the instructions. To the unwary observer, the appearance was that Transkei was voluntarily taking a free decision to vote on the issue of Transkeian independence. The innocent observer was also duped into believing people were divided on the issue, and the existing divisions were reflected in the two parties in the Legislative Assembly. One, the Democratic Party, was led by the veteran politician, Chief Victor Poto. The other party was led by the up-and-coming K.D. Matanzima, a relative newcomer in the Transkeian political scene, but one who carried the mantle as chosen pilot for the nascent Bantustan state. His party was the Transkeian National Independence Party.

Against all predictions, Chief K.D. Matanzima's TNIP won the vote comfortably. This result was not a reflection of the strength or weakness of any of the two leaders. It was not a case of the pro-independence party having won the debate or having made a good case. The voting cattle who supported independence had not been swayed by any argument, but were merely following instructions. If they had been ordered to vote for Timbuktu or Ouagadougou, they would have done so without caring or bothering what Timbuktu or Ouagadougou meant.

What their vote meant or implied, these traitors did not care, so long as they had done their duty, namely, obeyed instructions. The pattern for the future had been set. The government party would always achieve what it wanted, and what the people or the world thought or felt did not mean a thing. Many visitors and observers had descended on the Transkei to witness or monitor this "historic event", while ordinary Transkeians went about their ordinary chores, hardly giving the matter a thought. Experienced observers remarked it was clear the ordinary people had not been fooled and were not joining this circus. In the towns, the government organised celebrations; otherwise, there was a visible absence of any displays of spontaneous mirth and happiness from the people themselves.

Even before the organised mirth was over, the government was already engaged in its dirty tricks campaign. An agent provocateur, a White man whose name is unknown to the author, was busy trying to trap members of the opposition. At first, he had been hobnobbing with Chief K.D. Matanzima and TNIP members. After barely two weeks, he claimed to have become disenchanted with Chief K.D. Matanzima and his myopic followers. According to him, they were beyond redemption and their ties to the NP were too strong. In fact, their programme had been prescribed for them by the South African Cabinet. He confided that Chief K.D. Matanzima was the biggest stumbling block to African emancipation.

One evening, after dining out with some leading members of the opposition, he asked if someone would lend him a firearm as he was going somewhere and had no firearm. He expressed shock on learning they had no firearms and had applied for them without success. He won their trust and confidence after finding and supplying them with firearms, although unlicensed. He said he was determined to do good for the people of the Transkei and would find the means to bump off K.D. Matanzima. He did not wish to involve any Transkeian in the plot, but would ask his friends only to help him with some cash, but to leave the rest to him.

He showed determination to ingratiate himself with the Thembu sovereign and spent a lot of time trying to inveigle the sovereign to hand him some money. Sabata was always wary and suspicious and was never with him alone. He never gave him a cent for his schemes and ventures. Two Democratic Party heavyweights, Nkosiyane and Nogcantsi, took the bait and gave him the money he asked for. Their conversation with him was taped and used as evidence against them when they were charged with "conspiracy or plotting to kill Chief K.D. Matanzima". They were sentenced to long prison terms and their political careers effectively terminated. Yet again, the Thembu sovereign frustrated the vile conspirators and escaped from their clutches.

Chapter 19

Matanzima, the autocrat

Transkei's "independence" was hardly a year old when Chief K.D. Matanzima picked a quarrel with the Methodist Church of South Africa, a church with the biggest following in Transkei. The quarrel was artificial, contrived, completely uncalled for and unnecessary. Little men who had no real battles to fight conjured up disputes just to impress their followers. It became a game of: "What can happen if the big man is annoyed?" The Transkei government banned the Church in Transkei, inconveniencing and hurting thousands of innocent churchgoers. The pretext for taking action was that "the church was hostile to and contemptuous of the Transkei government". What had the church done to incur the wrath of Chief K.D. Matanzima?

To give the full story and its background, one has to go back to the early years of NP rule. Soon after coming to power in 1948, one of the first tasks of the D.F. Malan government was to offer to take over all mission schools and colleges. This move was directed chiefly at the mission schools that were run and controlled by the churches. Fearful of the government's sinister intentions, the Methodist Church of South Africa had declined the government's offer. With the passage of time, the church had realised that it was unequal to the task and did not have the resources to carry the onerous burden. Belatedly, it approached the government and offered to hand over the schools.

The government agreed in principle, but said it would send its own evaluators to determine the price the government would have to pay. When the valuation had been completed, the government referred the matter to the Church. Before any payment had been made, Transkei had become independent and the church list included schools that were now under the new Transkei government. The church had to take the matter up with them. When the Transkei government was asked by the Church to pay, they felt embarrassed, as they did not have the money. At first, they prevaricated while asking the South African government to help them out.

The South African government was still dodging and ducking when the year came to an end and the Methodist Church held its annual conference. At the end of the conference, greetings and good wishes were usually sent to the government. When this point was reached at the conference, one cleric asked if the greetings and good wishes ought not to be sent to the new Transkei State as well. Questions were raised about the genuineness of the so-called Transkei State and a discussion followed about the other nascent states in the pipeline. The Church felt it should leave out the greetings and good wishes. Less bother, it was said.

When news of this reached Chief K.D. Matanzima, he pretended to be outraged and insulted. If that was the attitude of the Church, then it was not welcome in Transkei. This was a smart and clever way of closing the question of when and how the government proposed to pay for the mission schools. By this petty and cheap trick, Chief K.D. Matanzima mishandled a delicate matter and caused the Church and its many congregants great distress. When Major General Bantu Holomisa and his Military Council took charge of Transkei's affairs in 1988, the matter was dealt with harmoniously and expeditiously and to the satisfaction of everybody concerned. It is amazing how the actions of one selfish and self-centred individual can impact negatively on the lives of many innocent people.

If there is one episode which exposed the dark side of Chief K.D. Matanzima's character at its worst, it was the Joyi affair. Chief Mgubhuli Joyi of Mputhi in the Mthatha district died young, and his younger brother, Zwelibhangile, acted as regent while the heir, Marhelane, grew up. Marhelane completed his studies at Lovedale during the Second World War. Joyi, the progenitor, had been Thembu regent while Mtirara's son and heir, Ngangelizwe, was a minor. The Joyis are senior chiefs and high up in the Thembu hierarchy. Chieftainship had been frowned upon by the White government and only the Paramount was accorded royal status. Thus, Zwelibhangile was treated as headman of Mputhi.

Marhelane never took over from his uncle, Zwelibhangile. He was not interested in being headman. He was far happier and contented working as a farmer and agriculturist. When Zwelibhangile died, Marhelane stood back and another uncle, Mthawelanga, had to act as headman. Years later, when Mthawelanga died, people were hoping Marhelane would at last come forward and take over. Marhelane said he had not run out of uncles and now it was the turn of his uncle, Zanengqele, to be headman. Zanengqele was the father of the stormy petrel, Twalimfene. Marhelane's eldest son was already circumcised and therefore of age to be headman if asked. However, he had not been asked.

One would have thought all this was of concern to Mputhi residents only. It had nothing to do with the population at large, least of all the Transkei government. Evidently the Matanzima duo, Chief K.D. Matanzima, the President and his brother, George Matanzima, the Minister of Justice, thought otherwise. It was George Matanzima, who started poking his nose into Joyi affairs. In the light of later developments, it can be said for certain that he was not acting on his own, but had been set up by his elder brother K.D.

It was George Matanzima who invited Marhelane to see him at his government office. Marhelane responded to the call and was surprised when the Minister said he wished to get some information as to what was happening at Mputhi. Puzzled, Marhelane asked, "In connection with what?" The Minister then narrated the above story, underlining what appeared to be Marhelane's adeptness at sidestepping every opportunity to take over as headman of Mputhi. He ended with this comment, "You do not seem to be interested in the position, which is rightly yours, but you have never come out openly to say so. Throughout my lifetime, there has been an acting headman at Mputhi and what I would like to know is, acting for whom?"

Marhelane tried hard to control his annoyance and succeeded. He asked politely, "But why should that concern you?" To this, the Minister replied reassuringly, "As Minister of Justice, such matters are of concern to me." Marhelane was unconvinced and replied disarmingly, "I would have thought you had more serious matters to attend to, instead of investigating petty parochial happenings of no national importance." Turning on his best charming look, the Minister smiled and countered, "I have called you my uncle, because of my high regard for you. As a senior in the Thembu hierarchy, you should not be living in colourless anonymity. With you at the head of Mputhi, you would also be in the Dalindyebo Regional Authority and, therefore, in the Transkei Legislative Assembly. With your education and natural ability, you would be in the cabinet if you did the right thing, joined forces with those trying to build the Transkei nation and cut ties with the malcontents and negative forces who always find fault and criticize."

The meeting did not end on a happy note as Marhelane did not show interest in all this. When George Matanzima had finished talking, Marhelane asked coldly, "Is that all you wished to say?" When the Minister said, "Yes, but I was hoping to hear your reply." Marhelane looked tired and said softly, "I do not want to say anything and will ask your leave to go." He got up and was shown out. The Minister must have given a report of this meeting to his elder brother, the president. The next step in this saga was taken by Chief K.D. Matanzima in person. He arranged for Mrs Joyi, wife of Mvuzo, the younger brother of Marhelane, to be brought to him. Mvuzo was teaching in the Mthatha district and had his own homestead in Mputhi. He had a fine figure and athletic built, reminiscent of his youthful days, when he was one of the promising middle-distance runners in Transkei. Marhelane, his elder brother, did not compete in the track events in his youth, but was a competent and stylish high jumper.

It is reported that Chief K.D. Matanzima first sounded out Mrs Joyi, on the likelihood of her husband responding favourably if offered the chieftainship at Mputhi, which implied being head of the Joyi dynasty. It must have been a case of "great minds think alike", and Chief K.D. Matanzima must have struck a responsive chord with Mvuzo's wife. Mputhi residents were rudely disturbed in their quiet and unsuspecting complacency by the news that President K.D. Matanzima would install Mvuzo as Chief Zwelidumile Joyi at Mputhi on a given date.

The Mputhi people found the sheer effrontery of the whole thing mind-boggling. Was Matanzima stark raving mad? Who was he and by what right did he dare pick somebody to be their Chief? It was up to the Joyis to say who their head was. Common decency required the authorities to respect the views of the Joyi family in such a matter, as well as the feelings of Mputhi residents. The president had no *locus standi* in the matter. Mputhi in the Mthatha district was in the domain of the Thembu Monarch Sabata, and Matanzima, a Chieftain at Qamata, had no say in the matter. He had also by-passed the Dalindyebo Regional Authority. Was this petty Chief from Qamata above the law and now a law unto himself?

Could it be that Matanzima had been misled by the rantings of sycophants such as Mthuthuzeli Lujabe, his Minister of Foreign Affairs, and Theo Mcinga, an announcer at Radio Transkei? The two had coined up the absurd translation of "His Excellency" when referring to the president as "Omfezeko igqibeleleyo", which had connotations of infallibility and holiness. This seemed to have gone to Chief K.D. Matanzima's head and he took it to mean he could do no wrong and nobody could question his actions. Acute observers were saying, "The deluded fellow has forgotten he is human and imagines he is God's younger brother."

Throwing all caution to the wind, and eager to demonstrate that the Thembu monarch had become a non-entity, even in his home district, Chief K.D. Matanzima went to Mputhi to flaunt his powers and installed Mvuzo as Chief. In the face of this extreme provocation and gratuitous insult, Mputhi residents showed commendable restraint and admirable self-control. There was not a single act of breach of the peace. They did not try to disrupt the proceedings; they just did not show up and took no part in the silly circus.

Chief K.D. Matanzima's show of force did not win people's hearts and minds for Mvuzo, who remained isolated. Mvuzo, as appointed Chief, called meetings at his place, but people did not attend. Rather, they went to the Great Place, his father's place, which now was Marhelane's homestead. The standoff continued until, in despair, Mvuzo went to Chief K.D. Matanzima for advice and assistance to turn around the Mputhi residents. Chief K.D. Matanzima could only think of drastic action and advised accordingly.

The upshot was that 50 Mputhi residents were arrested and detained for two months without charge. After two months of detention, they were released, but two of the so-called ringleaders were banished. Marhelane was banished to Mtingwevu in the Cofimvaba district and Dalagubha to Mahlungulu in Qumbu. True to the adage that power corrupts and absolute power corrupts absolutely, Chief K.D. Matanzima was now going from one wrongful and stupid action to the next. Dalagubha challenged his banishment in court and was partly successful. It was held to be unconscionable to confine him to Mahlungulu, where he could not find work to support himself and his family. The banishment from Mputhi was upheld and he could only visit Mputhi with the prior consent of Chief Mvuzo, the Mthatha Magistrate or the Station Commissioner.

Marhelane did not challenge his banishment to Mtingwevu. He spent a relatively short time at Mtingwevu and just disappeared; his whereabouts was unknown. What irked Chief K.D. Matanzima was to find that Marhelane's family was getting on well and did not seem to feel the effect of Marhelane's absence. This was annoying. Again, it had been expected that Dalagubha would go to the labour centres to seek employment, but instead it was said he had sought and found shelter at Sabata's Great Place at Sithebe. Mvuzo complained that Dalagubha was too close for comfort. He said there was a regular procession of visitors from Mputhi to Sithebe and Dalagubha was masterminding his continuing boycott from Sithebe.

Finally, Chief K.D. Matanzima approached the Thembu sovereign and acquainted him with the complaint. He also asked the sovereign to tell Dalagubha to find accommodation elsewhere. The sovereign countered by saying his position did not allow him to do such things. He was protector, not persecutor. The Great Place was not just his private residence, but more importantly, it was the home of the homeless and refuge for fugitives. Nobody could be turned away from the Great Place. Even the one who was complaining about Dalagubha was welcome to come and stay if he felt the need.

Evidently, Chief K.D. Matanzima felt Dalagubha's case could wait, but Marhelane's had to be dealt with urgently. On a Friday, a police van turned up at Mputhi and headed for Marhelane's place. They were accompanied by two open trucks and a bulldozer. They told Mrs Joyi, Marhelane's wife, that they had come to remove her and the family to Mtingwevu. They started loading the furniture and household goods onto the trucks, while Mrs Joyi was trying to console her distraught family.

While this was going on, the Joyi's second-eldest daughter, Pumeza, who was a teacher at Buntingville, arrived, intending to spend the weekend at home. She was devastated at the sight.

When the loading was complete, the bulldozers got to work demolishing and smashing the buildings and razing them to the ground. Others began torching the stock kraals and setting them on fire.

Just when they thought their work at Mputhi was finished and they were about to order everyone to get on board for the trip to Mtingwevu, Marhelane's livestock arrived from the commonage. What to do with these cattle, horses, goats and sheep was the question. Mrs Joyi was now told to remain behind to handle the difficulty of finding custody for the livestock from neighbours. The whole problem was left to a lone woman, as the sun was setting. The daughter, her protests ignored, was ordered onto the trucks. Mrs Joyi was left amidst the smoldering ruins of her homestead to do the best she could. Pumeza did her best to show a brave face and did not shed a single tear. She said she did not want to give the family's tormentors the satisfaction of seeing her break down.

It was only at Mtingwevu, after the police had left after dumping them at their "new home", that she collapsed and sobbed uncontrollably for some minutes.

We return now to Dalagubha and his safe haven, the Thembu Great Place at Sithebe. Chief K.D. Matanzima had not given up and decided to approach the Police Commissioner, Lieutenant Cwele, to use his good services. Matanzima found Lieutenant Cwele unwilling to do the dirty work. Cwele did not wish to do anything that would infringe the honour and dignity of the Thembu monarch. Chief K.D. Matanzima was compelled to bide his time and turn a blind eye on Dalagubha. In due course, Lieutenant Cwele retired and Martin Ngceba was appointed as his successor. Martin Ngceba of the Qoma clan was a Thembu national. One would have expected him to be no less solicitous of the honour and dignity of the Thembu court than Cwele.

When Chief K.D. Matanzima asked Colonel Ngceba to rid the Thembu Great Place of the pest that was Dalagubha, Martin Ngceba lost no time. One early morning, residents of the Sithebe Great Place were startled to see Dalagubha being pushed rudely to an awaiting police car. They alerted the Paramount who came out fuming, "How dare you?" Two men grappled with the sovereign to prevent him from rushing to the police car. They were pleading, "We won't let them have you! This is a plot to get you." Meanwhile, Martin Ngceba was driving off with Dalagubha as captive. Martin Ngceba had not had the courtesy to report to the sovereign and request his permission to take Dalagubha away for questioning.

What Cwele refused to do over many years, Martin Ngceba accomplished in one morning.

Years later, Martin Ngceba's turn would come and he would find himself awaiting trial in the police cells in Idutywa. Finding that he was to sleep on the bare cement floor, he begged for a mattress in view of his status. Martin Ngceba had forgotten something, but the supposedly dumb and dull policemen had not. Years earlier, one Transkei cabinet minister, Ndzumo, had fallen foul of the ruling party, and in line with their viciousness, Ndzumo was arrested and kept in Idutywa cells. When Martin Ngceba asked these policemen to provide him with a mattress, they saw fit to remind him and asked him pointedly, "Did you provide a mattress for Ndzumo?"

The so-called common people notice everything and miss nothing. Dalagubha, the man who was roughly handled by Ngceba, was one of the seniors in the Thembu Royal House. He was son of Zwelibhangile Joyi, Marhelane's uncle and regent. Prince Dalagubha was years later to act as regent for the absent son of Sabata, Buyelekhaya. At a time when it was dangerous to defy Chief K.D. Matanzima, the house of Joyi frowned upon his pretensions and refused to bow before the impostor. It was Regent Dalagubha who handed over to Buyelekhaya, Sabata's son, the heir to the Thembu throne.

Chief K.D. Matanzima never showed any remorse and never apologised for his wrongdoing and cruelty to the Joyis, even after the homelands had been disbanded. For his 80th birthday celebrations in 1995, Chief K.D. Matanzima wanted all the Dlomo clan to attend. President Nelson Mandela begged the Joyis to attend, saying this was the best opportunity whereby he would arrange a private get-together, where all differences could be ironed out and apologies made. They were prepared to forgive if K.D. Matanzima showed contrition and tendered an apology.

In the event, there was no private get-together at Qamata and Chief K.D. Matanzima made no peaceful overtures and expressed no regret. The Joyis felt they had been taken for a ride. Nelson Mandela was the guest speaker and, in his speech, he rebuked Chief K.D. Matanzima for his former excesses, without referring to the Joyi affair in name. This did not go well with the Matanzima family nor the other guests. It was felt Nelson Mandela's strictures were out of place and the timing inappropriate. People deplored Mandela's mishandling of the matter. Even procedurally, he was wrong. He should have brought Chief K.D. Matanzima to Mputhi where he should have made his apology for his misdeeds. Nelson Mandela could have endorsed Chief K.D.'s apology and asked the Joyis to accept the apology. That was the correct way of handling the rift and curing it. No reconciliation was made and Chief K.D. died without making any amends and more is the pity.

The Mpondo Paramount Botha Sigcau died in 1978, leaving his son and heir, Mpondombini. The late Paramount had been Chief K.D. Matanzima's close associate and helper in the formation of the Transkei Bantustan. One would have thought Chief K.D. Matanzima owed him some loyalty and that the Transkei government would support Mpondombini. For reasons best known to themselves, the Transkei government tried to revive Nelson Sigcau's claim to the paramountcy. What the motivation behind this campaign was, one can only guess. It would appear it was a cheap bid for popularity and, at the same time, a clumsy attempt at kingmaking. In all probability, Chief K.D. Matanzima was eager to win the gratitude of amaMpondo by being the person who had finally succeeded in restoring the legitimacy of the Mpondo monarchy.

The Minister of Foreign Affairs, Mthuthuzeli Lujabe, was the special envoy sent to Mpondoland by the Transkei government after the death of Botha Sigcau. Lujabe made it a point to ask Nelson Sigcau to state who was next in line to take over as head of the Mpondo nation. What he hoped to achieve is anybody's guess. Nelson Sigcau of course was no fool and could place no reliance on support for his aspirations (if he still held them) on unreliable and questionable sources such as the Transkei government. Replying to Mthuthuzeli Lujabe, Nelson Sigcau blandly replied, "It is my brother's eldest son, Mpondombini." Of course, that was not the answer Lujabe had hoped for and wanted to hear. Nelson Sigcau had not given the Transkei government a grip to hold onto. Mthuthuzeli Lujabe was not sure what advice to give to his president.

The Mpondo succession would remain unresolved for years while the Transkei government was busy fishing in troubled waters. It now transpired that after the death of Mandlonke in 1938, his widow had had a son, according to "Ukungena" custom (whereby a senior brother takes as wife the widow of his brother), with the putative heir, Nelson Sigcau. This son, Zwelidumile, was at Ndimakude in the Flagstaff district and had married Chief K.D. Matanzima's daughter. Now the Transkei government engineered and started a campaign on behalf of Zwelidumile. The rationale for this campaign was that as progeny of *Ukungena* union, Zwelidumile was *de jure* a son of Mandlonke and therefore had a stronger claim to succession than Mpondombini. Strangely, amaMpondo appeared unconcerned in this contest, while the Transkei government was busy trying to garner support for Zwelidumile.

Despite their apparent lethargy, when crunch time came and amaMpondo had to decide by vote, they unhesitatingly gave their overwhelming support to Mpondombini who became Paramount with the royal appellation Chief Thandizulu. The unsuccessful manoeuvring did not endear Matanzima to any section of amaMpondo, but reinforced the traditional Mpondo wariness of the wiles and guile of abaThembu (amakroloni). We can regard this duplicity and unscrupulousness on Chief K.D. Matanzima's part as proof that there is no honour among the thieves.

Of the countless examples of lawlessness and disregard for proper channels, Chief K.D. Matanzima was guilty of, one example in particular stands out. Retired Magistrate L.H.D. Mbuli was appointed Chairman of the Public Service Commission. Matanzima had now become used to abusing his position and authority by badgering the members of the commission to appoint his nominees. They found this practice disagreeable and unpleasant, but nevertheless remained compliant to the president's dictates. Evidently, Chief K.D. Matanzima had come to take the compliance of the Public Service Commission for granted.

One day, a telephone call came from the president intimating who they should appoint. On this occasion, his call had come too late: the matter had already been dealt with and the appointment decided. Mr Mbuli was hurt and annoyed and felt Matanzima was making fools of them and ignored the request. In a follow up, Matanzima raised his concern that his suggestion had apparently been overlooked. Mr Mbuli then explained the intimation from the president had come late after the matter had already been resolved. Matanzima was not satisfied and inquired what difficulty there was in doing some juggling.

Mr Mbuli had objected and asked the president not to make things difficult for them. The president did not take kindly to this and felt Mr Mbuli was getting too big for his boots and was now teaching him how to behave. If that was the way he showed his gratitude to him, for appointing him to that coveted post, then he was going to show him who was who. Piqued, Matanzima suspended Mr Mbuli with full pay and appointed somebody else to the post. Mr Mbuli spent his last two years drawing his salary, but doing no work. He was careful not to stray very far from Mthatha lest a call should come requesting him to report for work. He was never called and completed the two years, getting money for jam. Matanzima did not care. After all, the money was not his.

This was not an isolated case, nor the result of a passing aberration. It had become accepted practice. There was neither the machinery nor means to call Chief K.D. Matanzima to book. It was not that the transgressions were not known. There was no way to redress the wrongs. He had this impunity.

Chapter 20

Greed and graft

What about the greed and the graft? Do we just gloss over those and simply say, "Does it really matter?" No, the story must be told in all its ugliness. It would be a shame to hush-hush the matter. It has always been accepted practice that no gifts or presents should be accepted or taken by government ministers or public servants as reward or payment for the performance of their duties. Any gifts or payments received are deposited in the consolidated Revenue Fund. In the case of Transkei, Chief K.D. Matanzima took it upon himself to revise and review this practice. He found the practice to be unjust and oppressive.

His justification for the decision to allow gifts and presents to be made was that it was a recognised and acceptable Xhosa way of expressing gratitude and appreciation. Added to that, royalty and chiefs in general have from time immemorial been honoured that way and it was wrong and an insult to refer to such payments as bribes. That now became the accepted code of conduct in Transkei. Chief Matanzima's way of doing things was never to throw the matter up for debate. He would, after evidently spending a good night somewhere, wake up with a brainwave. He would see no need for any discussion and his thoughts would be made law.

As he had the final say on the allocation of fixed property, appointments to government posts and also dispensed grants and other favours, Chief K.D. Matanzima was to become the receiver of presents, gifts and money on an unprecedented scale. To handle the large volume of incoming mail and flow of gifts, two people were occupied full-time daily, sorting the mail, counting and recording money and presents. The two were government employees, but the money and presents belonged to Chief K.D. Matanzima. The money was deposited in Chief K.D. Matanzima's banking account and the Consolidated Revenue Fund got nothing.

When Chief K.D. Matanzima was about to retire, he went on a tour of Transkei, visiting all regions to bid the people farewell. These were organised functions to shower the president with presents. There were many public buildings and institutions that bore K.D. Matanzima's name, including the Mthatha airport. He had not contributed a cent towards those buildings and had not donated a chair. He was always recipient, but never donor. It seemed the fellow was truly mean and lean. He just got his name plastered at no cost to himself, but to others.

It can be stated without fear of contradiction that Chief K.D. Matanzima was handsomely paid and did not have to resort to this shady practice. The scale of pay of the Transkei president was on par with what the presidents in the Western world received. At Chief K.D. Matanzima's instance, the salaries paid to Paramount chiefs were raised to equal what the cabinet ministers received. For good measure, Chief K.D. Matanzima ensured that he was promoted and also made Paramount chief. Thus, the Qamata wonder kid was receiving two fat cheques at top notch level. Always careful to feather his nest, Chief K.D. Matanzima piloted a bill in the Transkei parliament providing that, once retired, the president's stipend be converted to a pension payable for the rest of his life. The provision became law.

It was also provided that, upon retirement, the president took the presidential car as his own. Six months before retirement, Chief K.D. Matanzima got a new presidential car, so that on retirement, he should take home a car as good as new.

Were the ethical standards of the Nationalist government any higher? Let us see what the track record reveals. The South African government had sent Justice G.G.A. Munnik to Mthatha as a judicial prop to the Bantustan state. He was appointed Judge President of the Supreme Court of Transkei. Without a shadow of doubt, Justice Munnik was a brilliant lawyer and competent judge. The only flaw was that he was sent with a political agenda and thus, good lawyer that he was, he revealed a shocking legal weakness.

Legal niceties gave way in his judgments to political expediency in a glaring manner. The case of the State vs. Mphopho is in a class of its own. The accused from Sterkspruit was charged with murder in Judge Munnik's court. The political overtones in the case arose from the fact that the case was one of those resulting from the deep divisions in Sterkspruit, following its forcible joinder to Transkei. Pro- and anti-Bantustan forces were at each other's throats and many killings had resulted. Mphopho was charged with the murder of a pro-government victim and appeared before Justice Munnik and two assessors.

In his judgment, Justice Munnik said he and his assessors had listened closely to the evidence given by the accused. Fortunately, the Judge said, one of the assessors was a Xhosa linguist, while he himself understood the language sufficiently to have followed what the accused was saying. Both the assessor and himself found the accused to be a liar and rejected his testimony.

The accused was found guilty of murder without extenuating circumstances. When the court rose, the Attorney-General approached Justice Munnik and told him the accused had not spoken Xhosa, but had given his testimony in Sesotho. Well, well, well, there you have it. The Judge and his assessors had followed and understood the Xhosa the accused did not speak! Surely that must be a world record. So, was the accused acquitted? No, the judgment stood. They appealed, but lost.

Chapter 21

The Sabata saga

The so-called Transkei Parliament was rambling on. It was a poor show, but its members took themselves seriously as if somehow their naturally-handicapped institution could by chance mature into a true parliament. The governing party was led by Chief K.D. Matanzima, who therefore regarded himself as above everybody else in the house, including the Speaker. The Opposition was led by Mr K.M.N. Guzana, a fine gentleman, with impeccable manners and a fluent English speaker with a fine turn of phrase. The overbearing attitude of Chief K.D. Matanzima was a severe handicap and a strain on the working of the house. He was even overriding the Speaker.

Mr Guzana, the Leader of the Opposition, appeared too gentle and soft and Chief K.D. Matanzima appeared to be taking advantage of this fact. Matanzima had never been a democrat and had little respect for interplay between government and opposition. What mattered to him was the simple fact that he controlled the majority. To him, debates were a waste of time and merely delaying the foregone conclusion that the decision would go the way of the ruling party. He had, and showed, respect to Mr Guzana in person. At Lovedale and Fort Hare, Mr Guzana had been his senior.

For most of the opposition members, he exhibited ill-disguised disdain and had difficulty controlling his impatience when they spoke. He treated the opposition as an unwelcome and wearisome nuisance. The Democratic Party and the opposition at large were not happy with the gentlemanly and polite approach adopted by Mr Guzana. K.D. continually hit below the belt and the opposition was tired of his bullying tactics. They wanted a leader who was rough and tough like K.D. himself. It was time K.D. got as much as he gave. At its next general meeting, the party elected Hector Ncokazi as its leader.

Hector Ncokazi was in the prime of his youth, uncompromising and hard-hitting. He had leftist views and little respect for Bantustan heavyweights like Matanzima. The scene was set for a real rough and tumble in the Transkei parliament. Chief K.D. Matanzima had other ideas and was not prepared to enter into political wrestling with a "disrespectful communist" like Hector Ncokazi. Using his wide powers, he had Ncokazi banned and then detained so that the Democratic Party became leaderless.

Pending its next general meeting, the party executive appointed senior leader Paramount Sabata as acting leader. This was something the Thembu did not like as they felt it was cheapening Sabata.

After Sabata had been inveigled to join the Transkei Legislative Assembly, his three remaining districts, namely Mthatha, Mqanduli and Engcobo, became members. The Transkei Legislative Assembly was not a democratic institution. It consisted of 100 members, 60 of whom were traditional leaders. They were members and representatives of tribal authorities. It was the remaining 40 who were elected by popular vote. Thus it was that tribal authorities had a built-in majority in the Transkei Legislative Assembly.

This lopsided arrangement was made by the apartheid government, the creator of the Bantustans. As the Bantu Authority members were government appointees, the Bantu Authorities were, without exception, obedient and loyal to the apartheid state. So the Transkei Legislative Assembly was not a democratic institution.

In the Transkei parliament, Chief K.D. Matanzima was top dog and the Leader of the Opposition seemed like an impetuous irritant. It was not proper for the Thembu Paramount to be under Chief K.D. Matanzima anywhere, anytime. His presence in that Chamber served the interest of the apartheid state and not his Thembu people.

The Bantustan setup was to trap Sabata, not in the so-called parliament, but outside its walls. In the course of his duties as Acting Leader of the Opposition, the Thembu Paramount attended a meeting at Qumbu in 1979. In his address at the meeting, Sabata said the government had dropped its mask and was acting openly as a police state. Now that it had discarded its camouflage, it was acting viciously and with abandonment. He said that the description of Transkei as an Independent State was a sick joke. Everybody now was feeling the pinch, except for the NP's boss boy, Chief K.D. Matanzima. Sabata said even he was treated like any other "*kaffir*" and was Thembu monarch in name only.

He said he was now trampled upon even in his own home, the Thembu Great Place. He told the meeting about the arrest of Dalagubha and said the police officer had not even knocked, nor asked for permission to enter. Freedom in the Transkei was for Chief K.D. Matanzima alone and not for other people: Transkei had become a large prison. Paramount Sabata was not given to extravagant use of language and even here he appeared to have chosen his words carefully. There was no hyperbole, no falsification of facts. What he said was the plain, if unpalatable, truth. Of course, in those times, truth was regarded as a dangerous weapon, but the Thembu Paramount was no ordinary person.

Nobody at the meeting had been perturbed or feared any dangerous consequences. Even when the Mthatha grapevine reported K.D. was furious at the insult and considering action against the Thembu monarch, people were not alarmed. In fact, they were laughing and saying, "So, the truth hurts." When, in fact, the Paramount was charged with insulting and harming the dignity of the president, people could hardly believe it to be true. Truth is stranger than fiction. In the abuse of power, the targeting of political opponents for persecution and harassment had become a specialty. Many bad and cruel deeds had been perpetrated. One could be excused for believing that nothing could still surprise anybody. There was a prevailing climate of fear and doom, but even in that atmosphere, it is an understatement to say the news that the Thembu Paramount had been charged by Chief K.D. Matanzima was a shocker.

Even the most wayward and unscrupulous usually stop short of certain actions. Nobody had ever imagined that the wicked K.D. Matanzima would go as far as that. Certain things are just not done. For several years, Matanzima had been engaged in acts of disrespect to the sovereign Sabata, bordering on open rebellion. The Thembu monarch had suffered all the insubordination and impertinence with amazing goodwill and forbearance. If there was someone who was guilty, numerous times, of committing acts that were an affront to the other, it was K.D. He had been doing so with impunity for so long that it was now apparent he had come to believe he had the right to despise and insult the Thembu monarch. It was a gratuitous insult to the monarch to charge him with showing disrespect to Matanzima who, in truth, was the king's subject.

To compound matters, K.D. was head of the ruling party, the TNIP. As such, he was right in the political arena and not above politics, as the presidency required. What was worse was that he abused his power as Transkei president by meddling in tribal affairs and even local matters. A case in point was the Joyi affair and his taking it upon himself to appoint Mvuzo as chief at Mputhi. If one castigates the TNIP and its leader for high-handed and meddlesome conduct, this was construed as an insult to the president.

The Thembu Paramount was the acting head of the opposition Democratic Party and had made the "offending remarks" in that capacity. He was discussing political issues and had highlighted outrageous acts by government officials. To illustrate that even traditional leaders were feeling the pinch, he mentioned the case of Dalagubha's arrest. He explained that this wrongful and unlawful arrest was committed at his Great Place and that the police officers did not even bother to ask for permission to enter.

The Democratic Party should have come out fighting, ready and determined to raise hell. Unfortunately, after years of ceaseless battering at the hands of the merciless Chief K.D. Matanzima, the party had lost its vigour and seemed to have even lost the will to fight. It had been softened and almost emasculated. It looked puzzled and at a loss about what to do in the circumstances. They could only whimper that Matanzima was treating them unfairly and making the work of the opposition impossible. It was clear that they were not challenging him. It was as if they were disarmed and in an unequal contest, which in fact was true.

The government on the other hand was working up a frenzy of righteous indignation and injured innocence. The alleged slight or smear against the president was viewed in a serious light and equated to treason or *lese-majesty*. Members of the Democratic Party were not strenuously defending freedom of speech, free political debate and the right to differ. They were almost apologetic in their approach, even suggesting that in political rallies, a slip can be expected and it was possible for one to err.

They appeared to be appealing to Chief K.D. Matanzima's good sense and understanding. It was not a wise move and was almost admitting that a wrong had been committed, but that it should be condoned. With this muted and half-hearted defence, the initiative remained with the government. If the Thembu monarch had blasphemed or uttered words that were anti-Christ, he could have gotten away with that easily. To offend His Excellency, the President of Transkei, was the biggest sin and an unpardonable sin at that.

There was no precedent for what was taking place and both those who were for and against were charting new ground. Nobody had ever been as big and as important as this Ozymandias,[56] the President of Transkei. The ordinary Thembu folk, on the other hand, could not comprehend this silly pretence. Who was insulting who? This was another Nongqawuse! The very idea that the Thembu monarch was an accused, and Chief K.D. Matanzima, the king's subject, was the accuser and complainant, was something out of this world.

The situation had been turned on its head. Who was Matanzima to call the monarch to court? Didn't Matanzima owe loyalty to his sovereign? Was Matanzima no longer a Thembu that he could be allowed to entertain these treasonable ideas? Yes, in the so-called Transkei state, Chief K.D. Matanzima was president and head of State, but

---

56 Ozymandias was reputedly the Egyptian pharaoh, Rameses II – "King of kings", as he called himself in Percy Bysshe Shelley's famous poem. Online: https://www.poetryfoundation.org/poems/46565/ozymandias [Accessed 30 November 2018].

did that entitle him to despise and show disrespect to his monarch? It was the NP that had created this mess and it was the Thembu people and their monarch who were suffering.

The question that nobody could answer was why Matanzima had found it necessary to harass the Thembu monarch. After all, he was now the unchallenged master of Transkei and the Thembu monarch was no impediment in his path. Added to that was the fortunate circumstance that the Thembu monarch had been big-hearted and magnanimous. He had been able to swallow, or simply ignore, all the indignities and invasions of his honour and status that Chief Matanzima had indulged in all these years. One would have thought it would be difficult to hate a good person, but in this case, it seemed to arouse Matanzima's ire even more.

The most probable cause would seem to have been envy, pure and simple. Chief K.D. Matanzima had power and was feared even by those who detested him. The Thembu monarch, for his part, had a natural charm and was universally adored. In that, he had no equal. In his presence, K.D. paled to insignificance. The Bantu Authorities Act had been touted as a mechanism for the restoration of Bantu honour, pride, tradition and values. In the first Bantustan territory – Transkei – all it had done was to raise the stipends of the heads of the tribes and to render them powerless. It had elevated as their master an upstart, a petty chief from the Thembu nation. Instead of restoring Thembuland's pride and honour, Bantu Authorities had dismembered the Thembu nation and left it in tatters; and forced its monarch to flee to exile in 1980.

The case of the Thembu Paramount has not been given the attention it deserves. No head of the Thembu nation had been hauled before a court of law on a criminal charge and not because they had all been models of good behaviour. As head of the nation, the sovereign was held in high regard and his dignity and honour protected. In handling cases of transgression by the sovereign, great care was taken not just to protect the person, but the monarchy itself. In the case of King Sabata, there was never any need for damage control. There was the good fortune that he was a person of exemplary character and whose conduct had done much to enhance the dignity and honour of the monarchy. His whole life never had the slightest shadow of criminality.

His first brush with the law, the alleged insult to His Excellency, the State President, was a politically-contrived charge with no moral opprobrium. It was not the law enforcement officers who took the matter up, nor was it the general public who felt aggrieved. It was strangely the president himself who, in his cheap conceit, was offended. The charge against the monarch was a thinly-disguised political persecution that should have been thrown out by any self-respecting prosecutor. However, any state prosecutor who had done that would have placed himself and his career in jeopardy.

A state prosecutor in the Transkei at the time, if he knew which side his bread was buttered, would have known that the best way to handle the matter was to ignore what the law required and do what K.D. wanted. That was the "Alice in Wonderland" that Transkei had become. It was unpleasant and degrading to have to do somebody's dirty work, but then one could only pity the poor mortals in this cruel and dirty world. The poor things could not be choosers. Theirs was to obey and do as instructed or starve.

The political situation in Thembuland was bleak. After the Thembu Paramount had joined the Transkei political circus and become a member of the "Transkei Parliament", he had gradually neglected his own court, which progressively became less important. He now spent more time in opposition party politics. He had not carried to the opposition benches even the members of the house of Dalindyebo. Big names in the royal house such as Chief Justice Mtirara, the heir to the Regent Jongintaba, were members of Matanzima's TNIP. Sabata's own half-brother, Chief Bambilanga, was likewise in the TNIP.

In the event, he could no longer count on the undivided loyalty of even the Dalindyebo Regional Authority, many of whom were sell-outs. As a member of the Opposition, the Paramount was like a deviant. In the Thembu house itself, he could no longer count on majority support. It was the Joyi house that was still solidly behind him. Even the Mgudlwas had become divided in their support. With the machinery of state behind him, K.D. was now more favoured and although he was lower in the Thembu hierarchy, now even his seniors deferred to him. They seemed to depend on him, not him on them, for patronage. No one dared contradict or stand up to him.

When news broke that the Paramount was facing criminal charges, there was hesitation as to who should call a meeting to report to the nation. Finally, some councillors called the meeting and announced to shocked listeners that a Thembu, Kaiser Daliwonga Matanzima, a descendant of a junior house of Mtirara, had done the unthinkable and taken the monarch to court. A committee was appointed to liaise with the Paramount and also to raise funds for the defence of the case. A day later, a decree was issued by the president's office prohibiting any soliciting or raising of funds for the defence of criminal activities like insulting the President. A serious warning of grave consequences to those people associating themselves with such criminal actions was issued. People raising funds would be charged as *socii criminis*.

Judged by any standard, K.D. had gone too far. This was unheard of. Unluckily, the opposition was already too tame and quiescent. It did not mount a challenge to the draconian edict. Instead they were asking, "Can this sort of thing be legal?" It is true that in Transkei at the time, nobody could say for certain what was lawful or unlawful or what was permitted or disallowed. With the leaders themselves nonplussed ordinary people were baffled and did not want to risk and challenge Matanzima's decree. There was a persistent feeling that K.D. was wrong, bluffing or just chancing his arm. Everybody felt the decree was unjust and repugnant to the principles of natural justice and equity. However, meetings for the defence stopped in their tracks and no fundraising took place.

It was as if a helpless victim had been left to the mercy of a lynching mob. As a result, the Thembu sovereign found himself deserted, alone and left to his own resources to fend for himself as best as he could, unassisted. To prevent any demonstration of support and solidarity, the venue of the trial was shifted from Mthatha to far away Port St Johns in Mpondoland. This would also ensure that Thembu nationals would find it difficult to flood the court during the trial. Evidently, the vile conspirators wanted to commit their dastardly act out of sight, undisturbed. They were now prepared and ready for the kill. Things were moving with the inevitability of a Greek tragedy in an eerie atmosphere of impending doom or cataclysmic climax.

In Transkei, the Thembu sovereign was held in high regard by all and sundry. He was the most beloved and respected of all the traditional leaders. He also had good relations with all the royal houses and all privately found that what K.D. was doing revolting. No one, however, was prepared to stand up and say so and risk annoying the president. It was crunch time and no one was prepared to rub K.D. up the wrong way.

To salve their consciences, they found a convenient way out, namely, to say it was best to leave the matter for the Thembu themselves to sort out. Alas, the Thembu nation was stupefied and hamstrung.

As if this were not bad enough, it was announced that the Judge President G.G.A. Munnik himself would preside over the trial. Ordinarily, that would indicate that the case was regarded as important enough to call for the best. Those who had given Justice Munnik's track record a closer look knew at once that the Thembu monarch did not have a snowball's chance in hell of an acquittal. That in itself sent shudders down the spines of those who knew the Transkei judicial setup. No anti-government accused was allowed to escape punishment in his court. So, the Paramount's fate was sealed.

Now that the Transkei president himself was the complainant, people feared the only point left to determine would be the degree of guilt and the appropriate penalty in the circumstances. In truth, the honourable course – and Justice Munnik himself knew it – was that he should have recused himself. The personal relationship between the Transkei president and himself, the Judge President, placed him in an invidious situation. It is true that when he came to Transkei, his specific assignment was to prop up and bolster the Bantustan government. If he declined to preside over the case, would he perhaps be guilty of dereliction of duty? Definitely not, as the Transkei government was already by that time firmly established and the opposition defeated.

Moreover, K.D. was pursuing this case for petty personal and spiteful motives. It was solely for his ego and had nothing to do with concerns of state or security. Since no state security concerns were involved, Justice Munnik should have felt free to recuse himself. His close ties with the Transkei president precluded him from making an objective and impartial finding. This was an important case against the head of the Thembu nation, involving Matanzima who had been waging a vendetta against the Thembu sovereign for years already.

Common decency and his own self-respect should have compelled him to step aside. With the Thembu monarch's future in the balance and his impeccable enemy baying for his blood, Justice Munnik should have made it possible for him to get a fair trial. He should have averted the danger of a political agenda obtruding and influencing the course of justice. However, Justice Munnik succumbed to the weakness of human nature and the easy temptation to help a friend, in this case, President K.D. Matanzima. In so doing, he not only boosted Matanzima's vanity, but also inflicted incalculable harm to the Thembu people and their long-suffering sovereign.

In the president's close circle, there was no one with an independent mind or sufficient clout who could tell K.D. to stop the madness. These sycophants were all vying with each other, trying to impress the Transkei president with their disgust at "Sabata's rudeness". Instead of quenching the flames of anger, they were stoking the fire. The South African government was the only authority who could call K.D. to a halt. They were hardly likely to do so in this case. They had found the Thembu Paramount difficult to handle and had little sympathy for him. They might even have been glad to see him worsted.

Of course, they knew that petty and personal vengeance was cheap and bad politics. For all that, in the final analysis, they would not want to deny their friend his morbid satisfaction. Like true politicians, they would say they could not see their way clear to interfere in a Transkei domestic issue.

As expected, the court ruling at Port St Johns found the Thembu monarch guilty and sentenced him to a fine of R700 or 18 months in prison. Ex facie, he got off lightly, but that was the appearance and not the reality of the situation. He had a harrowing experience in court where he was stripped of his royalty and handled like an ordinary "*kaffir*" facing a criminal charge. K.D. had achieved his main purpose, which was to humiliate Sabata and trample him in the dust. The gruelling cross-examination, as well as the baiting by the court itself, had exacted a heavy toll. It wore Sabata out and shook his self-confidence. The case had been a vivid demonstration that he was nothing and Matanzima, sublime.

The amount of R700 was meagre, but that was not the point. What really mattered was that he was now a convicted criminal and a court of law had made him an underling and K.D. his superior. The true purpose of the charge and conviction had been to teach him who-was-who in Transkei. It was fervently hoped he had learnt a salutary lesson. If only they knew that instead of being penitent and contrite, Sabata had found even more reason to intensify the fight against the White supremacist government and its Bantustan henchmen. He regarded the trial, verdict and sentence as a travesty of justice. It was all a gross insult.

He was dumbfounded and disappointed at the subdued and low-key response of the Thembu people to the trial and its outcome. By and large, abaThembu had behaved like a nation of cowards and the monarch must have felt let down. It was indeed a sorry spectacle. The good-natured, clean-living and kind Thembu sovereign was now a convicted criminal. The very thought was so outrageous it was unbelievable. To think that all this was at the instance of a man who had committed openly many acts of assault, arson, malicious injury to property, as well as other acts of cruelty, was just unacceptable. To add insult to injury, this brazen criminal was held up as a symbol of righteousness and probity. He was even referred to as "His Excellency" and had never had to answer for any of his multifarious transgressions. His sanctimonious rectitude was not only a provocation, but an insult to people's intelligence. One was reminded of the saying, "Truth forever on the scaffold, wrong forever on the throne." It seemed those who spoke of "this mad world" were right.

The Thembu monarch appealed both the verdict and the sentence. Many people believed there was enough room for both Matanzima and the Thembu Paramount. It now appeared K.D. believed it was time for one or the other and the weaker had to go. Of course K.D. had not spelt out what his full agenda was, but actions spoke louder than words and his actions indicated he now wished to liquidate the Thembu monarch. He had sent a clear signal that the monarch was now at his mercy and, of that, he had precious little.

The Thembu monarch, with his good nature, had been prepared to live and let live. In his otherwise unblemished life, he now found himself standing in the way of an ambitious and unscrupulous man. For his part, the monarch had been accommodating, but it appeared the new bull wanted no rival or potential rival. It was in this hostile climate that the Thembu monarch made a difficult and unexpected decision – to turn his back on the land of his birth. The concatenation of events precipitated a crisis and a decision had to be made, not sooner or later, but at the time. Even those who refused to accept the reality and believed only what they saw with their own eyes, could no longer pretend they did not see that Bantustan freedom was a big lie and that oppressions had intensified considerably.

It is said K.D. was gloating and self-satisfied. He felt those who accused him of spitefulness and cruelty to the Thembu monarch had been proven wrong, as his actions had been vindicated by the court. People were holding their breath and anxiously wondering what Matanzima's next step would be. Had he reached his goal was he still pressing ahead and should people prepare for still more to come?

Very few people knew the Thembu monarch had decided to go into exile and the king's departure caught the nation by surprise. Long after he was gone, many people were still asking what had happened or if it was true that he was in hiding. Now that he had gone, the question was: would he be allowed to return? More pressing was the worry about what would happen to his family. Would they be allowed to live their lives in peace and who would look after them? What people feared was that no one would take up the responsibility for their upkeep and general wellbeing. It was never even imagined that Matanzima would go out of his way to put a squeeze upon them and systematically ensure they were miserable and on tenterhooks.

As soon as K.D. received the news that the Thembu Paramount had left the country, he lost no time in taking over the Dalindyebo Region's affairs. He became the self-appointed director and arbiter of the region's affairs. It soon became apparent that the hounding of the sovereign and forcing him into exile was not the end, but the beginning of the programme. He was now to keep his long nose deep in Dalindyebo affairs. He sent his premier and brother, George Matanzima, to approach the Dalindyebo Regional Authority to find out "what steps they proposed to take against the fugitive from justice, the convicted Sabata".

The dispirited and disheartened members of the Dalindyebo Regional Authority were caught unprepared and had not yet discussed the matter. The premier said he would wait while they went to caucus. Hoping to appease both the premier and, more importantly, the Transkei president, they agreed to impose a fine on the Paramount.

They had decided to pay the fine from their own contributions. The premier rejected the suggestion and emphasised the gravity of the offence and said the president would not accept anything less than the Paramount's suspension. To prove their loyalty, they readily agreed and passed a resolution suspending the Paramount in view of the conviction. The poor fools did not know the powerful weapon they were handing to Matanzima. They were mere pawns in a sinister game that had consequences they did not yet comprehend.

Armed with the suspension of the Paramount, K.D. now moved into top gear. The Transkei president announced that the position of Thembu Paramount had become vacant. He did not stop there, nor indicate that the matter was in the hands of the house of Dalindyebo to decide on interim measures. He did not leave the matter in the hands of the Dalindyebo Regional Authority for their consideration. Instead, he made a shocking and defamatory pronouncement, alleging that in fact Sabata had been an illegitimate posthumous child, whose biological father was unknown. He was an impostor, and not the son of the Thembu monarch, Sampu.

The gratuitous insult to the Paramount was treasonable and an unpardonable affront to the Thembu people as a whole. The sheer effrontery of the imputation put him beyond the pale. At least a raving lunatic does not know what he is doing and cannot be held responsible for his insane utterings or doings, but Chief K.D. Matanzima could not plead insanity, nor a slip of the tongue; his utterings were deliberate and premeditated. This gross insult was a thousand times more serious than the mild comment about him for which Sabata was crucified. It should also be remembered that Matanzima never retracted or apologised for the injury to the name and reputation of the Thembu monarch.

Nobody challenged Matanzima for his treasonable statement. Seeing that no challenge was forthcoming from the house of Dalindyebo, K.D. was emboldened to go further. He did not want nor did he ask the house of Dalindyebo for their views on the way forward. Instead, he announced that he was proclaiming Chief Bambilanga, the eldest son of Nonciba, junior wife of Paramount Sampu, as the true and rightful heir of Sampu and, in consequence, successor to the vacant throne. It was only quietly and in private that voices asked, "And who the hell are you to decide who Sampu's heir should be?" Nobody from the Thembu royal house or the Dalindyebo Regional Authority questioned Matanzima's *locus standi* or his right or title to decide on the matter. They all sheepishly acquiesced.

K.D. had not only overthrown the Thembu Paramount, but had also removed his progeny from the line of succession. He had, by right of might and abuse of power and authority, erased the reign of Sabata, as if it had been a mistake. Matanzima's nominee, Chief Bambilanga, knew K.D. was talking through the back of his trousers. He knew he was an impostor and was being used by Matanzima in furtherance of the latter's agenda.

Right or wrong, however, he didn't care, but was thankful for the opportunity to bask in the glory of the position and also enjoy the benefits and perks due to the incumbent. All this amorality reminds one of a sermon delivered by the Reverend H.L. Henchman of the Presbyterian Church at Alice. In 1940, he had the temerity during a sermon at Lovedale College to say, "I sometimes wonder whether you Natives have any sense of honour." The students could not shout him down or walk out and did what they could safely do to mark their displeasure at what they regarded as a gratuitous insult. They shuffled their shoes noisily on the floor and coughed incessantly.

When the Paramount Bambilanga stepped into Sabata's shoes, he moved into the official residence at Sithebe and, in so doing, evicted Sabata's junior wife, NoCanada. At Bumbane, Sampu's Great Place and residence of Queen Novoti, Sabata's mother, it was NoMoscow who was in residence. Although they would have loved to force her out, they could not do so openly and had to rely on indirect means, like frequent raids at all times of the day and night under the guise of checking if there were no terrorists or fugitives from justice sheltering at the Great Place.

The distress and discomfiture suffered by his family must have been relayed to the exiled monarch and affected him adversely. Now that his stipend had ceased, his family had no income and was living in strained circumstances. His life in exile was stern and rigorous, but it was the want of funds of his own and the reliance on charity that was difficult to bear. The collocation of events must have had a traumatic effect on the Paramount and shortened his life. The news from home was most disheartening, with not a glimmer of hope.

The life the Paramount was experiencing was like a nightmare, but the nightmare may have been endurable if there were some indications that the apartheid fortress was under siege and crumbling. There were no visible cracks even in the Bantustan and it appeared he would never be able to return home and would never see his family again. With no sign of victory, there was no hope and with no hope the will to live, dies. It came as no surprise when the news came that the Thembu monarch had passed away in Lusaka, Zambia, on 7 April 1986. Matanzima's Transkei looked impregnable and K.D. was bestriding the Transkei like a colossus. Of all the Bantustan leaders, he was the most pompous and self-opinionated and thought he was a cut above all others. His territory was bigger, his population more numerous and he could almost believe that Transkei was a country in its own right – with him at the very pinnacle.

Believing the past was gone and forgotten, the grief-stricken family wished the body of the Thembu monarch to be brought home for burial at his home. There was no certainty that K.D. would allow the request, but surprisingly, he allowed the request without difficulty. The Dalindyebo family met to prepare and arrange for the funeral. Chief Bambilanga was also present and when it came to the consideration of the necessary repairs to the Bumbane Great Place, he asked to be counted out. He willingly left the question of all arrangements and, in fact, the funeral itself to the keen and enthusiastic volunteers who were eager to foot the bill.

Enthusiasts countrywide sent messages of support and pledged financial contributions. It soon became apparent that the funeral would be a big affair. Matanzima stepped in and said he was taking charge of the funeral and the arrangements. The body was already in Mthatha and had not been brought there for Matanzima to toy with. He issued a proclamation closing the Transkei borders to all vehicles coming to the funeral. No repairs were permitted to be made to the Bumbane Great Place. The family was excluded from all arrangements. It was reported K.D. contented Sabata and had been deposed. He would not allow that he be buried with the honours of a sovereign.

Finding that they were in an impossible situation, the widows NoMoscow and NoCanada brought an urgent interdict before the supreme court of Transkei restraining K.D. from holding the funeral. They also requested the court to authorise the return of the body to Lusaka for burial as it was not possible to hold a decent and respectable burial in the Transkei. The urgent interdict was applied for and granted on Saturday, the day before the Sunday appointed by Matanzima as the date for the funeral.

The order was served on Chief K.D. Matanzima at Chief Bambilanga and Gwiliza's funeral parlour, where the body was kept. The widows and their families breathed a sigh of relief now that K.D. had been prevented from carrying out his plans and making a parody of the funeral. For a change, they slept restfully that Saturday night. Very few people were aware of the application and the interdict. The few who knew went to church that Sunday morning in a happy mood and in fine spirits. There was inner satisfaction because "Feleba" (Chief K.D. Matanzima's nickname) had been interdicted from holding the funeral and making a cynical mockery of the affair. It had been cause for much concern and suppressed anger that "Feleba" was succeeding in his plans to bury the Paramount as a nonentity. The interdict was preventing a national disgrace.

According to reliable reports, when the interdict was served on him, "Feleba" shook his head. After the sheriff had left, it is said he enquired, "I wonder who is advising these poor women to challenge me? Do they imagine they can succeed where their husband had failed?" Chuckling, he continued, "Are they seriously hoping that this piece of paper can stop me?" From that careless remark, he was revealing how far gone he was. As far as he was concerned, the law was meant for other people and not him. Still, the cynical contempt for legal process was unexpected and was unbecoming of him, a qualified lawyer.

On the Sunday morning of the funeral, K.D. arrived at Gwiliza's Funeral Parlour in Norwood, Mthatha, with an entourage of seven cars. In his company were police officers and security personnel. There was no one in attendance at the funeral parlour and an officer was sent to go and fetch Mr Gwiliza, who came to the parlour and in defiance of the interdict, opened and delivered the Paramount's body to Matanzima. Chief Bambilanga was also present.

The body of the Thembu monarch was placed at the back of an open van. It was not conveyed in a hearse, as "Feleba" felt it did not deserve even that little respect. It lay at the back of the van like a bag of sand. There was nobody sitting beside the coffin.[57] A clerk, who had been present during the application, found it hard to believe when told what "Feleba" had done. Finally, he said, "The man is tough. He is impervious even to a court interdict." On arrival at Bumbane, the coffin was put down in front of the house and opened so that those present could see the body. From there, the coffin was carried to the bottom of the garden. The spot was not the burial site for the Dalindyebos. Digging had already been done and the coffin was lowered without any funeral service, ceremony or anything of the kind. After covering the grave, "Feleba" and his party departed. Throughout this sordid performance, the family was weeping from afar. They took no part in the proceedings.

The people present were to say later that they had witnessed a bizarre and obscene occurrence. In their words, what they saw was weird, a spectacle, as if Judas Iscariot was burying Jesus Christ. On most things, people have different and conflicting views. On that day's happenings, their views were unanimous. They expressed horror and dismay at an avowed enemy taking over a funeral in order to demonstrate his undying hatred and contempt for the deceased and in order to deny the bereaved family their wish to give the deceased a decent funeral.

---

[57] This author had the misfortune of observing this, as he happened to notice K.D.'s convoy that Sunday driving to the funeral parlour and followed.

In Chief K.D. Matanzima's long catalogue of evil deeds, this ranks as one of the most contemptible. On that Sunday morning, he plumbed the very depths of depravity. However what about Chief Bambilanga's role in this sordid affair? He paid an exorbitant price for Matanzima's favour in granting him the Paramountcy. If it meant he had to connive, nay, actually be an accomplice in the dishonouring of his brother, he should have found the price too high. What his true feelings were is anybody's guess.

As senior in the Dalindyebo family, he was custodian and protector of the family and its welfare. It was his duty to see to it that his brother, Sabata, had a fitting and decent burial. It was his obligation to render all assistance and support to the family of the deceased. When K.D. said he was taking over the full responsibility for the funeral, its preparation and arrangements thereof, he was in fact posing a challenge to Bambilanga. By failing to stand his ground and tell "Feleba" that this was a Dalindyebo family business, he betrayed the family. If there was a clash of interests between what "Feleba" wanted and the wishes of the family, his bounden duty was to see to it that the wishes of the family prevailed. What is even worse is that he not only tamely complied with Matanzima's decisions, but actually became an accomplice. This complicity on his part led to indecision and weakness by the other members of the family.

It took a lot of courage on K.D.'s part to carry out his diabolical scheme. It was his moment of triumph when the coffin was placed in the yard at Bumbane and nobody challenged him. As he directed operations at Bumbane Great Place, the lion's den, as it were, with those members of the Dalindyebo family present, voiceless and unprotesting, he savoured the moment, as the *de facto* Paramount of all of Thembuland.

He felt great relief that he did all he wanted to do without any visible opposition. He said, on the way back to Mthatha, "It had all been a great success and there hadn't been a single hitch." It was a fact that not one person rose in ungovernable rage to challenge K.D. for his audacious insolence. So he was pleased with himself and had a smug smile on his face and the satisfaction of a job well done. As subsequent events were to show, "Feleba" was quite right in believing he could treat a court interdict with disdain and not suffer any consequences. Nothing happened and there was no follow-up for his contempt of court. He was a law unto himself.

There was a story doing the rounds, initially, that Matanzima had been willing to allow the funeral to proceed unhindered. It was suggested he was alarmed and changed his mind when he saw the countrywide response and interest in the funeral. All Matanzima's actions indicate otherwise. The more probable explanation is that the crafty and spiteful fellow disguised his true intentions until the body was safely in Mthatha and, effectively, in his power. It therefore appears the trusting and unsuspecting widows fell into a trap. They had not discussed any conditions with K.D. and had not asked for any guarantees. They just thanked him for allowing the body to come home.

In retrospect, it is clear Matanzima also wanted the body to be brought back from Lusaka so that he could complete his unfinished business. He had been feeling cheated because the Paramount had not received a prison sentence and, to cap it all, escaped his clutches at the last moment. Although K.D. had climbed to the pinnacle of power, he had never been able to get a firm hold over the monarch or him under his control. With the conviction and the sentence, he was not far from having Sabata at his mercy. He had been nursing a grudge all these years because the monarch had denied him his "*coup de grace*" by skipping the border and going into exile.

We cannot begin to imagine the feeling of utter helplessness and devastation felt by the family of the deceased. In good faith, they had approached Matanzima with their request. They were fearful he might refuse to allow the body to return, but had never even entertained the thought that he wanted the body for his own private agenda. Little did they know that in taking the trouble to bring the body back, they were giving him the chance to vent the venom of his spleen over the lifeless body. They wanted an opportunity to pay their last respects to a loving husband and a kind father.

They also wished to give the Thembu nation the opportunity to bury their monarch, for he was the first and last people's monarch. It was only in Lusaka that the dead monarch had a dignified memorial service. Dr Kenneth Kaunda, the Zambian president, and the Zambian government provided a steel casket in which the body was brought home. The body left Gwiliza's funeral parlour in a cheap rough-hewn wooden coffin. Matanzima and Bambilanga Mtirara owe an explanation as to what happened to the Zambian casket, which was a tribute from the Zambian government and the people of Zambia.

Since the arrival in Mthatha of the monarch's mortal remains, nothing was done to mark its presence. The opposition Democratic Party were quiet and well-behaved like good boys, which it seems they were. They did not have the guts to even hold a memorial service for their fallen leader. Questions remain unanswered. Where were they in his family's hour of need? Why did they fail to take up cudgels for the defenseless widows?

It is here that we find the true measure of the parlous state of Transkei politics at the time. From the time of the arrival of the body in Mthatha, the opposition remained cowed and subdued. Even as K.D. announced his decision to take over arrangements and preparations for the funeral, they did not raise their voices in protest. They did not kick up any dust as one would have expected. Unlike sharp and stinging politicians, they were more like respectful and forgiving Sunday school teachers.

One would have expected them to tell K.D. uncompromisingly, "You keep out of this. You can bury your TNIP supporters, but we bury our own." Since they were giving Chief Matanzima free reign to do as he pleased, one wonders why they still called themselves the opposition. What were they opposing if the president was acting without let or hindrance? In short, they made things easy for him. It seems the house of Dlomo, the Madiba clan, was also bereft of men. How could it be that nobody, but nobody, rose up in righteous indignation to challenge Matanzima's profanity?

He dared them as he defiantly brought the coffin to the Bumbane Great Place and, in broad daylight, proceeded to bury his enemy like a dog. Why did the women's tears and the children's plaintive cries fail to goad the men to action? Guilt by default can also be as bad as the act of an accomplice. That is the final score.

It was to be a long wait and some years before the Thembu monarch's body was exhumed and reburied in a fitting manner and what a day it was! It was unlike any funeral before or since. In every way, it was a gala occasion, a day of jubilation and exultation for one and all. People in their thousands had come to make an emphatic statement. They were saying, "This is a man of courage and honour, of whom we are immensely proud." It was a befitting and truly uplifting demonstration. For once, everybody was happy and satisfied.

Chapter 22

Coup

How had the reburial of Sabata become possible?

Life is full of surprises and many twists and turns. While the people of Transkei seemed disheartened and resigned to their miserable lot, underneath there was some movement. It looked impossible to break the stranglehold which the Nationalist government and its puppet Bantustan Authorities had over the territory.

Relief was to come from an unlikely quarter. The Transkei Defence Force, which was primed to ensure tight control and prevent any uprising, was to provide the outlet. In a surprise move, it staged a coup that ousted Stella Sigcau's government.

It was Major General Holomisa and his Military Council who made the reburial possible, in an unexpected turn of events that caught the apartheid government unprepared. As much as they wanted to and hard as they tried, they could do naught to reverse the coup staged by Holomisa in December 1987. A direct military attack would result in a blood bath, with consequences too horrible to contemplate. They decided to swallow their pride and accept the coup as a fait accompli.

When K.D. Matanzima retired as president in 1986, his wish was for the Xhosa monarch to succeed him. It would be a big scoop for the government if even the intransigent Xhosa were seen to be finally toeing the line as obedient natives. If their monarch was willing to be used as a decoy by White supremacists, that would be a big plus for apartheid. What is more, that would vindicate K.D. Matanzima and exculpate him. If he was called a sell-out, then everybody was a sell-out.

The Xhosa monarch refused to be tempted and declined the offer. Interestingly, there were many amaXhosa in K.D. Matanzima's TNIP. As would be expected, they were praying and hoping their sovereign would be the next president. Hopefully, that would raise their status in the pecking order in the Bantustan. They never got the chance.

In the event, it was the Mpondo Chief, Tutor Ndamase, head of Nyandeni region, who succeeded Matanzima as president.

As the first president of Transkei had been the Paramount, Chief Botha Sigcau, it was in K.D. Matanzima's view undesirable that it should again be an Mpondo who should be president again so soon. He seemed to be concerned that it might put ideas into their heads and that they may come to believe that they were more deserving or even that it was their right. However, the Xhosa King, Xolilizwe, did not bite and it fell to another Mpondo to become the president.

The new president, Tutor Ndamase, was a mild and unassuming gentleman. With him as president, the post was merely ceremonial and he was content to live and let live. Because of his quiescent nature, he never even thought of changing the Transkei setup. He allowed things to remain as the apartheid masters in Pretoria and their Number One quisling in the Transkei had decreed. Therefore, it was business as usual, except that there were none of K.D.'s excesses.

Many wishful thinkers, simple and ignorant, fondly imagined that with K.D. Matanzima out of the way, it would be possible and easy to reverse Transkei's independence and rejoin South Africa. To their disappointment, they were to discover that it was not Matanzima, but the apartheid government who made and maintained the Bantustan state. Yes, K.D. Matanzima had become a power in his own right, but it was his will and determination, coupled with supreme ambition and confidence, that made the difference. Added to that, he had the unwavering support of his apartheid masters for any action he took. When he became president, he translated that to mean that he was supreme Chief of the Transkei and acted accordingly and no one had dared disobey him. George Matanzima, the Prime Minister, took orders from him and was happy with that.

When Tutor Ndamase was president, he did not give orders to the Prime Minister. By nature, George Matanzima was inoffensive and soft-hearted. He trusted and revered his elder brother and deferred to him always. He was, thus, never his own man and lived in the shadow of his elder brother. Politically, his views were moderate, but because he listened to and obeyed his strong-willed brother, his own views became inhibited. His own initiative found scope in areas like bugles and drums for schools and paraphernalia for drum majorettes.

All indicators suggest George Matanzima was happy and successful as an attorney, but unwisely agreed to be lured into politics where he was never at his best. There is a day to remember though, when he had his audience spell-bound. He was warming up to his theme and explaining his party's ties to the apartheid government and the audience was with him. He went on, "Many people criticize us and call us lackeys of Pretoria. Not at all and we will never be. One of our great thinkers, Dr W.B. Rubusana, once said, 'If you have to cross a river in flood, it makes good sense to ride even the Devil to get across. When you are on safe ground, you tell him, listen, pal, you go your way and I go mine.' We are doing just that and the day may not be far off when we tell the Devil to go his way and we go ours!" There was thunderous applause.

Later that same day, this author met three fellows who had attended the meeting and were still excited. They were extolling the cleverness of the Matanzimas in riding the Devil himself. The author jumped at this opportunity to disabuse the gullible souls. "You are actually rejoicing instead of shedding tears? Don't you know the meaning of the phrase, 'taken by the Devil for a ride'? Don't you know that that warns you that you are heading for the wrong destination? Who is Matanzima deceiving by pretending to be using the Devil for his own purpose when it is the Devil who's the master? And your shameless leader has the cheek to boast about leading the country on the Devil's back?"

They had stopped laughing and were looking at each other with puzzled expressions. The author was satisfied, hoping they would ponder and reconsider. Amorality and a lack of scruples had long been the bane of the oppressed. Many of their so-called leaders were smart alecs, who believed in being smart and clever rather than being principled and correct. A stage had been reached when honesty was openly scoffed at as a game for fools. Lamentably, George Matanzima's ride on the Devil was to have an unhappy ending. It was his elder brother who was to escape his due deserts till the very end. What a lucky one!

After George Matanzima's resignation in October 1987 following a corruption scandal, Stella Sigcau, the Mpondo princess, took over as Prime Minister. She was the daughter of the first president, Botha Sigcau, and had long been a member of TNIP. She was to have a short, but eventful stint in office. She did the unthinkable and very bold act when she had K.D. Matanzima arrested and locked up.

He was to spend two nights in custody before P.W. Botha, the South African Prime Minister intervened and instructed he be released and left alone. K.D. Matanzima was released and never charged. Observers and analysts were still trying to figure out if any real changes were possible with her at the head. Before they had any answers, Stella Sigcau was pushed out by a military coup that gave Pretoria many sleepless nights. Transkei residents were puzzled and confused and trying to assess its significance and figure out which way the wind was blowing. They were also trying to evaluate its potential.

During her short tenure as Prime Minister, Stella Sigcau had earned the accolade as "the doughty Mpondo maiden who castrated the fierce Thembu bull". Apart from that, there was nothing to earn our praise or gratitude. When she passed away in 2006, President Thabo Mbeki praised her profusely at the funeral as one who had excelled in the liberation struggle. Of course, we did not know which liberation struggle he was referring to. The Stella Sigcau we knew was a prominent member of the collaborationist Transkei Bantustan government. The people who should have been singing praises at her funeral were Messrs P.W. Botha and Pik Botha.

Chapter 23

King Sabata's reburial

The undignified and unceremonious manner in which King Sabata's funeral was handled by Chief K.D. Matanzima was a wrong that rankled and called for remedial action as soon as was possible.

Opportunity was to come from an unlikely source. During the rule of the Military Council headed by Brigadier General Bantu Holomisa, by and large, the shackles that bound Transkei people fell off. News came in 1987 that Prince Bambilanga had died after illness. Prince Bambilanga was the one chief K.D. Matanzima had singlehandedly foisted on the Thembu people as sovereign after Sabata had gone into exile.

Bambilanga's eldest son and heir, Zondwa, was an officer in the Transkei Defence Force and did not make any move. It is said it was K.D. who goaded him into action with the words, "Why are you not coming forward as heir and successor to the Thembu throne? Sabata was overthrown and you are the heir!" Zondwa then approached the Military Council with his claim, but was told that the question of succession would be decided by the Thembu people.

A Saturday was declared as the date for imbizo/national gathering, to decide on the succession. There had not been any mbizo in Thembuland for years and we did not know what to expect. We were also afraid that K.D., who had now been made supreme chief of a bogus "Western Thembuland", might come to the meeting as a bad influence. However, in the event, there was no K.D. at the imbizo and, except for the presiding officer, Chief Mveleli Silimela, the head of the Dalindyebo Regional Council, all speakers drummed on the fact that the heir had to come from Queen Novoti's issue and that Queen Novoti's son was Sabata.

The gist of all the speeches, therefore, was that Prince Buyelekhaya was the heir and there was no dissenter. It was by acclamation that Buyelekhaya was proclaimed the heir. Chief Mdanjelwa, who was brother of the head of the Dalindyebo Regional Authority, Chief Mveleli, was the preferred choice as regent for Buyelekhaya. The young prince Buyelekhaya had not yet returned from exile.

Part of the cleaning of the Augean Stables to prepare for the return to legality and normalcy was the popular clamour for the reburial of the late King Sabata. It was not just the two widows, NoMoscow and NoCanada, who felt aggrieved. All members of the Thembu royal house – in fact, the Thembu people as a whole and, surprisingly, the South African populace at large – were calling for a reburial of the Thembu sovereign.

That day did come and what a day it was! 1 October 1989. A day like no other! We had never witnessed such a vast concourse of people. It seemed everybody wanted to be there and to take part. The mood was joyous and celebratory. It was as if the people were not at a grim or solemn funeral, but in a liberty cavalcade. They were there to affirm their love, respect and fond memory for their beloved Jonguhlanga: the people's favourite monarch.

Everything went off well; from the funeral service to the warm tributes, even though many were not even listening to the formal proceedings, but busy rejoicing and dancing.

Most importantly, King Sabata was returned to his familial burial plot. K.D. had selected a spot for the king's burial away from the family graveyard, as if he was an outcast. The reburial brought him back and laid him next to his father, Sampu, and the other family elders.

The dissolution of Transkei as a bogus-independent state followed in a few short years, with reincorporation into South Africa in 1994.

Our eyes have not been closed and we have been watching unfolding events in the new South Africa. We have noticed former TNIP members, like the clever careerists and opportunists that they are, flock to the African National Congress, the new ruling party. Many have become ardent and vociferous comrades. It is as if there were no collaborators or traitors and we were all in the liberation struggle. What arrant nonsense! It has become fashionable in the new South Africa to distort history to suit party political ends.

On 15 June 2003, the veteran K.D. Matanzima passed away at the ripe old age of 88. It was generally expected that his family and friends would be left alone and given space to bury him as they saw fit. The House of Traditional Leaders at Bhisho, together with Congress of Traditional Leaders of South Africa (CONTRALESA), persuaded the Eastern Cape Provincial government to give the respected traditional leader an official funeral. When it became known that the leader of the Inkatha Freedom

Party (IFP), Mangosuthu Buthelezi, as well as Major General Bantu Holomisa the United Democratic Movement (UDM) leader, would speak at the funeral, the ANC government decided not to be outdone.

President Thabo Mbeki himself went to the funeral and, in his funeral oration, spoke warmly about the deceased. Admittedly, a funeral is no forum for attacking or belittling someone. That said, we were nevertheless aghast at the spectacle of leaders of the "democratic South Africa" lending respectability to a Bantustan despot and tyrant. As if that was not bad enough, they had the gall to lavish encomiums on one they should have shunned as a political leper. This was yet another indicator demonstrating how far the new South Africa has strayed from the true course of liberation. The saying is still true that, "Tell me who you go with and I will tell you what you are".

Chapter 24

Sebe debacle

During his heyday, K.D. Matanzima was entrusted by Pretoria with many missions and underhanded operations. At a certain point, Pretoria was unhappy with the dysfunctional Ciskei Bantustan and also became disenchanted with its Lennox Sebe. The fault was not with Lennox Sebe really, but with the inherently nonviable and unworkable contrivance that Pretoria herself had created as the Ciskei Bantustan. It was the White farmers who were unwilling to give up land for the projected Ciskei homeland, and, instead of addressing that issue, Pretoria chose to put the blame on Lennox Sebe's ineptitude.

In its plot to oust Lennox Sebe, Pretoria used Charles Sebe, younger brother of Lennox Sebe. Charles Sebe was in the Security Services and was highly regarded as intelligent, capable and efficient. In the event, the plot failed and Charles Sebe was arrested, charged and convicted and sentenced to 12 years' imprisonment. Pretoria pleaded in vain for clemency and presidential pardon. Later, South African agents sprung Charles Sebe and his accomplice from Middledrift Security Prison and whisked them to a place of safety in Mthatha. Pretoria was lying barefaced, suggesting this was a Transkei operation. Of course, K.D. Matanzima prized his ties with Pretoria more than his fraternal relations with Lennox Sebe and granted the requested asylum.

This in itself poisoned relations between Bhisho and Mthatha. More cause for straining relations further was yet to come. Their haven in Mthatha was used as a base from which the anti-Lennox Sebe elements could plot against him, while Pretoria was footing the bill for the Mthatha refuge. One morning, Lennox Sebe's presidential palace at Bhisho was attacked from the air and the mysterious plane flew away towards Kei Road. The attack was poorly executed and the damage minimal. The lie fed to the media was that the airplane was supposedly from the Transkei. However, there was a South African military base at Komga and they never spotted the plane both during its flight to Bhisho and on its return!

There were several stories bandied about, but the truth was never found out. One story was that Pretoria had hinted to K.D. Matanzima that Pretoria would look the other way and not see if K.D. decided to *bump off* Lennox Sebe and join Ciskei to his Transkei. The story goes that Pretoria wished to get rid of Lennox Sebe and his Ciskei.

They believed it would be a good idea to join Ciskei to Transkei with Matanzima as Head of the combined Bantustan State. Sebe's removal had to appear to be planned and executed by the "Bantu" without Pretoria's involvement.

The head of the Transkei Defence force was Colonel Reid Daly, a former officer in the notorious Selous Scouts of Southern Rhodesia.[58] He was appointed by Pretoria. It was suggested that he was willing to go along with Pretoria's scheme, but was unable to persuade his officers to agree to the venture. People on either side of the Kei were not willing to be participants in this unwanted, artificially-created "animosity" between Transkei and Ciskei. It was regarded as silly and stupid.

People were jolted from their lethargy by a news report of an army mutiny in the Transkei Defence Force. The story was that the officer corps had led a mutiny against Colonel Reid Daly. Events moved swiftly and we heard that the officers had pre-empted a plot by the Commander. They arrested him and prepared his expulsion order which was presented to the Prime Minister, George Matanzima, for signature. Armed with the signed order, they escorted Colonel Daly to the Transkei border and handed him to South African officers, safe and sound, with not a scratch.

Hitherto, the Transkei Defence Force had been an unknown quantity and the ordinary Transkeian hardly cared or knew much about it. It is true both Pretoria and the Transkei government had made much ado about the appointment of Zondwa Mtirara as Colonel Reid's understudy. This appointment was meant to endear the army to the people and to allay fears that the real reason for the army was to keep people under firm control and to crush any uprising; except that the said appointment was hardly likely to be reassuring to the people. After all, Zondwa Mtirara was the son of Chief Bambilanga Mtirara, K.D. Matanzima's henchman. Over and above that, nothing was known about the man himself.

Later, during a TV interview, Colonel Reid Daly could barely control his anguish and tears as he told of his humiliation at being driven through Mthatha's streets in the back of a van like a common criminal. For all that, in people's eyes, the mutineers scored full marks for their irreproachable conduct throughout the mutiny. Colonel Reid Daly had not been abused or ill-treated. There was pride and satisfaction that they were not a rabble, but a disciplined body of young men. Also, one cannot begrudge the ordinary people for enjoying basking in the glory of the unexpected success of their young men in ordering P.W. Botha's man to "voetsek".

---

[58] Southern Rhodesia became Zimbabwe in April 1980.

Having flexed their muscles, it was just a matter of time before these officers, after taking stock of the parlous state of the Transkei government, as well as the national situation, would stage a coup that toppled the government of Stella Sigcau in December 1987. She had spent a mere two months in power. Ordinarily, one would expect a military coup to be a retrograde step and a swing to the right. It would appear circumstances alter cases. Major General Bantu Holomisa and his military council introduced a benevolent regime and to a large extent relaxed the rigid control over people's lives and liberties which K.D. Matanzima had imposed. It was a great relief.

At the time, however, citizens had questions: Who were these army officers and what were their antecedents? We knew absolutely nothing about them, even as their names and identities were disclosed. Now with the advantage of hindsight, one is able to say unequivocally that their intervention was a blessing not only to the people of Transkei, but to South Africa as a whole. They were a fine crop of young men, well-trained not only in military code of conduct, but in self-discipline as well. One feels compelled to admit that Colonel Reid Daly should get some of the credit. That explains also his chagrin at what he perceived to be the base ingratitude from those he had given so much, to make and prepare to be true soldiers.

We had not completed digesting the military coup in the Transkei when we were overtaken by another coup in, of all places, the Ciskei this time. Are these things infectious or was someone imitating the Transkei experience?

The story sounded extraordinary and bizarre. Some inconspicuous brigadier bearing the harmless name, "*Oupa*" Gqozo, had staged a coup. What were we to make of this? Should we believe that, yet again, the Army Commander and Pretoria had been caught napping? It seemed too good to be true, but then again, there it was! We were flummoxed and unwilling to believe the news. How could this unlikely and unprepossessing "*Oupa*" Gqozo achieve, in a wink, what Pretoria had been unable to accomplish in years?

We were forced to the conclusion that this "*Oupa*" Gqozo was mighty clever, "'*n slim bogger!*". There was this nagging thought: "What will Pretoria and Charles Sebe do now?" The Commander of the Ciskei Defence Force was Colonel Anton Niewoudt, chosen by Pretoria, an officer in the Special Services, we understood. Had he also been outwitted by "*Oupa*" Gqozo? He must be a useless lout!

We were still mulling over this when it was reported that Charles Sebe and his companion, Onward Guzana, had been on their way from Mthatha to Bhisho, evidently to fish in its troubled waters, but had walked into an ambush. Onward Guzana was reportedly killed in a shootout. It was further reported that Charles Sebe had been wounded, but managed to escape and the hunt was on for him. Natural sympathy always goes for the underdog, in this case, Charles Sebe. We were praying and hoping he would elude his pursuers and escape. We were sorry for the dead Onward Guzana.

Alas! It was not to be. After many hours of anxiety, news came through that Charles Sebe had been tracked down to a homestead in the Gubevu locality at Zeleni and had been shot dead in cold blood. Oh, Lord! What a tragedy and unnecessary loss of life! We were almost stupefied now. This "*Oupa*" Gqozo was really a master schemer. How could the clever jackal, Charles Sebe, be caught so effortlessly in Gqozo's trap? What about his handlers and Pretoria? Had they also been caught flat-footed? We have been told many times (although we refuse to believe it) that truth is stranger than fiction. For "*Oupa*" Gqozo, it was all "Oh so easy!" We had to swallow that, though with some difficulty. After all a fact is a fact.

It was some days before we solved the mystery. We were the ones who had been fooled. Pretoria had not been out-manoeuvred and was firmly in control. "*Oupa*" Gqozo was not the loose cannon we thought he was. He was Colonel Niewoudt's and Pretoria's instrument! Although Pretoria regarded Charles Sebe as the best option, there were several cards up the Nationalists' sleeve. Pretoria had been ready to bide her time, but it was the Transkei coup that gave her the idea to look for their Bantu Holomisa in the Ciskei Defence Force. They picked on the inconspicuous, but likeable, "*Oupa*" and it worked. Having succeeded with the uncomplicated "*Oupa*" Gqozo, Charles Sebe became not merely redundant, but a veritable liability and therefore expendable. What better opportunity could there be than advising him to come over to Bhisho, and then tipping Gqozo off about Charles Sebe's trip and advising where to lie in wait for him? The job would be "*Oupa*" Gqozo's and Pretoria's hands would be seen to be clean.

All secret operatives work in that treacherous environment, where once one's usefulness is over, one is mercilessly killed or dumped. Better by far if they had allowed Charles Sebe to serve his prison term.

The new South Africa has been able to accommodate handsomely all apartheid's servants. With the much-lauded Truth and Reconciliation Commission, all has been forgiven. The leaders of the former Bantustans also have been allowed to live their lives in peace and all their pension benefits and packages safeguarded. "*Oupa*" Gqozo is the sole exception. He was discarded as a reject and thrown into the dustbin.

One expected the Truth and Reconciliation Commission to be even-handed in its approach. It did try and even Eugene de Kock was handled gently as he was being coaxed and encouraged to come clean and reveal all. Poor Gqozo was singled out for the harshest treatment. It was as if he was the worst creature spawned by abominable apartheid. One was reminded of the adage, the more things change, the more they remain the same. In South Africa, it is still a matter of show the White man respect and give the "damned Nigger" a good kick on his backside.

When it was P.W. Botha's turn to be called to the commission, he angrily dismissed the request. He was not subpoenaed and it was Archbishop Desmond Tutu who went to Wilderness to plead and humbly request if he would kindly agree to come to the commission. As expected, "*Die Groot Krokodil*" waved his index finger and rebuked him, "Don't come with that nonsense here!" And, of course, the matter was not pursued. To come back to poor Gqozo: he was made the culprit for the deaths of Charles Sebe and Onward Guzana. Everyone knows Colonel Niewoudt was "*Oupa*" Gqozo's senior and it is Niewoudt and Pretoria who bear the guilt for those deaths. Even with the Bhisho massacre, "*Oupa*" Gqozo's liability is less than Colonel Niewoudt's. It is unfortunate Gqozo has not come forward to admit he was a pawn in a game he did not even understand.

Chapter 25

AmaMpondomise

Tearing up the British umbrella

Let us take a cursory glance at amaMpondomise. No story of the people of Transkei would be complete without mention of amaMpondomise, one of the biggest tribal entities of the Xhosa nation. In the imperialist/colonialist version of history, amaMpondomise and their monarch, Mhlontlo, are vilified as trencherous villains who butchered the Qumbu magistrate, Hamilton Hope, and two of his staff in cold blood at Sulenkama in Qumbu in 1880.

We want to revisit the story of the rupture of good relations between amaMpondomise and the British and its tragic consequences. After the defeat of amaXhosa, the British were able to expand eastward, as well as northward. They were able to cajole abaThembu, amaXesibe and amaMpondomise to agree to be brought under the British umbrella "and thus protect their land from would-be predators". As a result of the agreement with Mhlontlo and his cousin, Mditshwa of the amaMpondomise, four magisterial districts were established, viz. Maclear, Tsolo, Qumbu and Mount Fletcher, as the territory was annexed to the Cape Colony.

In 1879, the British passed the Disarmament Act prohibiting Africans from possession of firearms. This was a restrictive and oppressive law to which the amaMpondomise and others had not consented.

The neighbouring country of Basutoland (now Lesotho) had lost much land through depredation by the Free State Boers. To avoid further loss, they agreed to British overtures to become a British protectorate. When the diamond mines were opened in Kimberley, they went there in numbers and, with the money they earned, acquired firearms for their defence. Disarming the Basotho was then the most urgent task for the British. The Basotho refused, resisted and fought back, and the Basotho rebellion of 1880 was on.

AmaMpondomise had cordial relations with the Basotho, their neighbours. In fact, in Mhlontlo's territory, there were Basotho communities. It came as an unwelcome and rude shock for Mhlontlo when the Qumbu magistrate, Hamilton Hope, told him that the British required his assistance in the war against Basutoland. He was required to open a front in the south-east with his warriors.

In fact, even before this request, Mhlontlo and his people were having second thoughts about "this British umbrella". The magistrates had come to Mpondomise territory as "the eyes and ears of the queen as well as her mouthpiece", which to the consternation of the amaMpondomise, were daily eroding their independence and sovereignty. AmaMpondomise were in a quandary as it now appeared that they could not just tell the British the experiment was over and that they should pack up and go.

The proposed fight against the Basotho was the straw that broke the camel's back. When Mr Hope broached the subject, Mhlontlo was evasive in his response. Fortunately, he had a genuine excuse: his wife had recently passed away and he was still in mourning. Mr Hope thought that that was a lame excuse and said so. Mhlontlo was offended, but replied calmly. He said he was surprised that the British expected amaMpondomise to enter the war with their assegais in a fight against an enemy armed with modern weapons. Let the British provide the guns. That was the challenge and Mr Hope agreed to provide them.

Now Mhlontlo was in a fix. AmaMpondomise were not exempt from the Disarmament Act. The British wanted to use them against the Basotho only to disarm them after the Basotho were defeated. Mhlontlo and his people were opposed to the Disarmament Act and felt that "the British protector" had no right to pass restrictive and oppressive laws against them. Mhlontlo was convinced that the time to part ways with the British had come. However, he decided not to part with the British empty-handed. He would await delivery of the weapons and take the guns and send the British home. Fighting to disarm the Basotho was not a good cause. In fact, it would be better to join the Basotho in their fight against the British.

Mhlontlo canvassed support for his rebellion against the British and thought he had won over the Mpondo monarch Mqikela. The Thembu monarch Ngangelizwe was a British loyalist like the "Fingos" (amaMfengu) and would not entertain the idea.

Next door to Qumbu was the Mpondo chieftain Nqwiliso at Nyandeni. He also would not bite. He preferred currying favour with the British.

Hamilton Hope agreed to meet amaMpondomise at Sulenkama to hand over the consignment of weapons. It is said he was aware of Mhlontlo's duplicity, but this was a battle of wits, as well as a test of wills. He thought wiser counsel would prevail and Mhlontlo would realise his weakness and stop short of his "mad venture". He was aware of divisions among amaMpondomise.

The situation was fraught with danger, but if he cancelled the Sulenkama meeting he would be a coward and his mission with amaMpondomise would have been a failure. He might as well pack up and go. It is true to say he was a courageous man in spite of his poor physique. He was lame in one leg. The Sulenkama events are history, but people differ in their interpretation. How did events play out at Sulenkama?

Cool and fearless, Hamilton Hope and his retinue entered the huge assembly and squatted in the front row of the circle facing the Mpondomise monarch and his councilors, seated facing them. Now let us see how they played their cards. It was the Mpondomise monarch who addressed the gathering without any preliminaries. There were ordinary tribesmen, but also warriors carrying assegais and shields. Mhlontlo said that everyone was aware that he was still in mourning and could not go to war. He said Diliza (Mr Hope's Xhosa name) was aware of that, but was still pushing amaMpondomise to go to war. He said the army would be led by his uncle Gxumisa. On the war itself, he said the person in charge was Diliza and that was the person they should listen to and whose instruction they should obey.

Having made his announcement, Mhlontlo called Sunduza, the son of Reverend Davis, the missionary at Shawbury, saying he had a message for his father. He led Sunduza out of the huge circle. They were some distance from the crowd and out of ear shot when, suddenly and without warning. Hamilton Hope and the two clerks were attacked and speared through the upper body with assegais. It was all over in a minute.

Mhlontlo was tried for their murder, but there was not an iota of evidence implicating him and he was found not guilty and discharged. Alas, he did not escape scot-free. Administratively, he was stripped of his kingship, banished from Mpondomise land and sent to Mhlahlane in Gatyana district among amaGcaleka. Even his descendants have not received any mercy. As the British put it, when amaMpondomise killed Hamilton Hope and the others, they killed their kingship. It was their own action. AmaMpondomise contend they were forced to act. It had not been spelt out what coming under the British umbrella entailed. The Magistrate, Mr Hamilton Hope, usurped the powers and prerogatives of their sovereign Mhlontlo. AmaMpondomise had not consented to surrender their independence and sovereignty. They were not British subjects and were not obliged to fight British wars, especially unjust wars against their friends and neighbours, the Basotho.

Atonement for Sulenkama tragedy

The reaction of the British to the Sulenkama killings was to inflict severe punishment on Mhlontlo and Prince Mditshwa personally. In addition, they confiscated Mpondomise land and settled White farmers on it. They rewarded those tribes (Hlubi, Bhele, Basotho and Bhaca) who had remained loyal and had supported them in the Mpondomise repression. Mpondomise land was ravaged and amaMpondomise displaced. Mhlontlo's royal residence was torched and razed to the ground and so was Mditshwa's.

Mhlontlo was on the run and was hunted till he escaped and found refuge in Basutoland. Mditshwa was arrested, tried and sentenced to prison. The aftermath of the Sulenkama killings was to be, for amaMpondomise, an unending nightmare.

In 1938, Prime Minister Field Marshal J.C. Smuts was in a predicament. The year 1938 had been the centenary of the Great Trek. Afrikaner nationalism and strong anti-British sentiment had been aroused. Extreme rightwing organisations had been formed and there was a strong anti-war propaganda.

The South African government was imploring the African community to come forward and assist in the war effort. Unlike during the First World War, when Africans had come forward eagerly, things had changed. The brutal policy of White "*Baasskap*" had alienated the African community. If they were not treated as citizens in peace time, they were not prepared to shed their blood for a government that denied them citizenship rights.

It was in this context that amaMpondomise took a bold decision. They shared the same sentiments of alienation as the rest of the African community. However, some among them felt it was incumbent upon them, in Great Britain's hour of need, to do something special to expiate Mpondomise guilt and atone for the Sulenkama killings. Prince Delibandla Mditshwa from the Gungqwane administrative area in Tsolo came forward with the idea that the time was ripe for an Mpondomise contingent to volunteer to assist in the war effort. This would erase the unpleasant memory of Hamilton Hope and his duo.

Perhaps amaMpondomise should have undertaken a public relations exercise and also apprised the office of the Chief Magistrate of their intentions. What happened was that Prince Delibandla Mditshwa and his volunteers turned up at the Magistrate's office in Tsolo and reported their readiness to assist in the war against Hitler. To the magistrate, this was a simple matter of military recruits. He was not aware of and did not see any diplomatic exigencies involved. After contacting the military depot in Mthatha, he advised them transport was coming from Mthatha to fetch them.

Somehow, something went wrong somewhere. The importance and significance of this Mpondomise overture was lost. There was neither official welcome nor any fanfare for these Mpondomise volunteers. The police camp on the banks of Mthatha River had been taken over by the Department of Defence and turned into a military base for the Transkei Battalion, whose commander was Colonel Fyfe King, a former chief magistrate. The experience of Prince Delibandla and his Mpondomise contingent in the army was most unpleasant. Because of his royalty, he expected to be regarded and groomed as an officer, but it was not to be. The Mpondomise contingent was not retained as a unit, but its members were just dispersed among the other recruits and lost their identity.

The rapprochement which amaMpondomise were attempting to initiate did not materialise. The expected thaw in the frosty relations between amaMpondomise and the government was not forthcoming. The venture Prince Delibandla made and the sacrifice the Mpondomise contingent was ready to make were all for naught. To the British and their heirs, the South African government did not mean a thing. I do not know what casualties amaMpondomise suffered in the war, but Prince Delibandla returned home safely and wiser.

As amaMpondomise say, the venture was undertaken to wipe the blood of Hamilton Hope and his companions and we say they did wipe that blood. If the British, after all these many years still bear the Mpondomise a grudge and refuse to let bygones be bygones, that is their own affair. As far as we are concerned, the Mpondomise can rest in peace with a clear conscience that they have done everything to atone for the Sulenkama killings of 1880.

Unending sorrow

Despite being a fugitive in Basutoland for many years, Mhlontlo's stay there was not all misery, stress and strain. His Basotho neighbours held him in high esteem and respect.

Again, after his banishment to Mhlahlane among amaGcaleka, the people of Mhlahlane regarded it as an honour to have the famous sovereign as their neighbour. Finally, he was allowed to return to Qumbu for his last few days. Although he was happy to return to his own, it caused him heartache to see how miserably the impoverished amaMpondomise lived under disdainful and haughty British officialdom. It was hurtful to be a powerless spectator. In their despondency, he encouraged them not to lose hope and to look for a better tomorrow.

When the beloved monarch died, he left a void that persists up to the present. His son and heir, Charles, was denied his rightful succession. The British insisted that when amaMpondomise killed Hamilton Hope, they also killed their kingship. Charles did not live long and died while still in his prime.

It was Masikizi, Charles's younger brother, who acted as regent and who lived to a ripe old age. He was acting for Charles's young heir, Sigidi. The missionary at Shawbury was Reverend Mears, a Christian gentleman in every way. He took under his care first Wabana Makaula, a Bhaca prince, together with Tutor Ndamase, the Mpondo prince. They stayed with his family like his own children. Shawbury had only a training school and a primary school. When the two completed their primary schooling, they went to Healdtown for their Junior Certificate. Reverend Mears then took the young Mpondomise Prince Sigidi under his care. I have met all three, Wabana, Tutor and Sigidi, and was struck by their good manners and humility. I was also able to meet Reverend Mears's eldest son, Gordon, who became Chief Magistrate of Transkei and later Secretary for Native Affairs. I also met the younger son, Walter, who was a principal of Rondebosch Boys' High School in Cape Town. Both were fine fellows with impeccable manners and spoke faultless Xhosa.

AmaMpondomise had high hopes for Sigidi, hoping he would redeem their fortunes and restore their status of parity with the amaMpondo and abaThembu for instance. The Regent Masikizi had done a good job, a good balancing act and maintained good relations all round. What had not been resolved was the impasse regarding the abrogation of the monarchy by the British imperial power.

Sigidi finally took over as head of amaMpondomise without the matter having been resolved. The 1948 elections had been won by Dr D.F. Malan's NP on an apartheid ticket. AmaMpondomise and their young leader were still fending off increasing pressure from the apartheid government, which was pushing hard for the acceptance of Bantu Authorities. Prince Sigidi had gone to Qumbu village when a coincidence of unfortunate events occurred. He was met by a tribesman who had returned from the mines and wanted to give the prince a present of a bottle of brandy and a case of beers. Because the law would not permit them to use the lounge of a local establishment, they and their companions decided to find a spot on the outskirts of town, under some trees. They were drinking when suddenly a police van appeared. The police had wide discretion in such matters. Depending upon the officer in charge, they could reprimand the offenders and order them off. This time, the officer in charge said they were arresting the group as offenders and ordered them to get onto the van.

The group was not drunk or noisy. The spot was quiet on the outskirts of the village. The police manhandled them as they were pushing them into the back of the van. In anger, the prince turned against one who had caught him by the collar of his jacket and struck him on the jaw, sending him staggering. The other policemen turned on the prince like a swarm of bees and knocked him down. They were in a rage and the prince was bleeding from the mouth, nose and a cut on the forehead when they threw him into the van.

All this happened in a short time. At the charge office, the group were given the option of paying admission of guilt fines – except for Sigidi. He was told there were several charges against him, including resisting lawful arrest and assaulting a policeman. He would remain in custody till his appearance in court. When the news of this calamity spread in town, people were shocked and perturbed. Some senior citizens who were in town went to see the station commander in an attempted damage control and to prevent exacerbation of racial tensions.

They asked the station commander to intervene and persuade the police to release the prince. The station commander pleaded he could not interfere with the legal process and that he was powerless. The following day, after the prince had spent the night in custody, a full-blown Mpondomise delegation turned up in Qumbu, with a request to see the magistrate. They told the magistrate that they were a peace delegation and their primary concern was peace and stability, to calm down racial tensions and that they wanted his assistance in that regard. The prince had to be released.

They said the police appeared to have overreacted in this matter. The prince and his followers had not disturbed the peace and were drinking quietly out of sight. The police could have ignored the technical breach or ordered them to leave. On the question of assault on the police, that was not denied, but the prince had struck one blow only. The police, on the contrary, had already meted out their own punishment. They had mercilessly battered the prince to submission. The charges against the prince should be dropped and they undertook to ensure, on their side, that amaMpondomise agreed to bury the hatchet.

The magistrate spoke to the station commander by phone, but the latter stood firm that the law must take its course. The prince was defended by Attorney J.G.S. Vabaza, himself an Mpondomise of the Gcaga clan. He had an office at Mthatha and at Libode. He handled the case with great skill and expertise. The verdict of the court was guilty on all counts and the sentence was six months' imprisonment. The court refused to suspend the sentence and the prince went to jail to serve his sentence.

That was not to be the last of their troubles. In the new South Africa, there was the Nhlapo Commission, which was set up to redress the wrongs of the past. The commission has focused on adjudicating the claims of traditional leaders and determining their legality, according to the law and custom of the tribe concerned. One would have expected that amaMpondomise would have had an easy go as their case was simple and straightforward.

Alas, it was not be. This time, we cannot blame the British imperialists or colonialists. They did not put in a word edgeways. AmaMpondomise were their own worst enemy. Three claimants to the Mpondomise kingship appeared before the Nhlapo Commission. It is reported that the three camps disagreed on everything, including Mpondomise history and even matters of fact, for example, that Mhlontlo was the last reigning Mpondomise monarch. They could not find any common ground.

Perhaps one should not have been surprised at the result. The commission could not find in favour of any of the claimants. With so many amaMpondomise in the legal profession, one would have thought any Mpondomise dispute would be a model of clarity of facts and issues. In the event, amaMpondomise produced what can only be described as a frog and crab dance, in the process of which the truth got lost.

One would have thought the two Dosini claimants did not have a leg to stand on. The Dosini had lost their seniority before the arrival of the colonisers and the Jola Clan became the royal clan. In the case of amaXhosa, the same thing had happened when Cirha was ousted by his younger brother, Tshawe. Similarly, with abaThembu, Hlanga, the rightful heir was overthrown by his younger brother, Dlomo. In these matters, no commission or court can interfere. It is the tribe concerned that has to deal with the issue.

In spite of the fiasco at the Nhlapo Commission, the Mpondomise picture is not all gloom and misery. King or no king, life goes on. It does not seem that the loss of kingship has been a handicap except perhaps over the question of Mpondomise sovereignty and territorial integrity. As individuals, they have not lagged behind other groups. As a matter of fact, in every sphere of human endeavour, they are to be found right in front, together with the best. They have many enclaves in Mpondoland and Thembuland and do not challenge Mpondo or Thembu authority. Throughout Xhosaland, they are found living as ordinary citizens with no fuss.

The redoubtable Xhosa general and statesman Makhanda alias Nxele was of Mpondomise extraction, a member of the Cwerha clan. He distinguished himself during the Fifth War of Dispossession [1818-1819] in organising Xhosa defence of the fatherland against British invasion. He became commander of the Xhosa forces and was in charge during the battle of Grahamstown in April 1819. In a bid for peace, he surrendered to the British later that year and was sent as a prisoner to Robben Island.

One would have thought the Mpondomise would have much to celebrate, but the poor Mpondomise have no national celebrations. Significantly, they failed even to erect a monument for their heroic sovereign, Mhlontlo. For their remissness, they deserve a good kick up the backside.

Chapter 26

Quo Vadis?

An elementary lesson reinforced by the ongoing history of royal houses, kings, queens, chieftainships and all their associated trappings is that the institution of traditional (tribal) rulership is not anywhere near its last legs. It has proven amazingly resilient and adaptable over time, due to its penchant for hunting with the hounds and running with the hares as the power balance swings hither and thither over the course of history. This has been the case in colonial times, the apartheid and Bantustan eras and the present.

While it could be argued that the major socio-economic paradigm of the current epoch is that of neo-liberalism (which foregrounds class relationships in society), group solidarities based on tribalism and its associated norms and rituals remain as strong as ever, in a world in which complex, multiple identities survive, if not thrive.

Interestingly, Archie Mafeje tells us that, "In South Africa the indigenous population has no word for 'tribe', only for 'nation', 'clan', and 'lineage.'"[59] He adds that, "In many instances the colonial authorities helped to create the things called 'tribes', in the sense of political communities."[60] Thus, it is a mark of false consciousness (his emphasis) on the part of those who subscribe to an ideology (such as tribalism) that is inconsistent with their material base and, therefore, unwittingly respond to the call for their own exploitation.[61]

Whatever view one subscribes to, there can be no arguing that the current South African regime is fully committed to the neo-liberal project. The institution of chieftainship was smoothly integrated into the "new South Africa" post-1994 and consolidated in the country's constitution. Thus, any "role" to be played by chiefs in the strategy of the ruling class would at least have to be consistent with the neo-liberal order or actually promote it. With land reform set to become a major policy platform of the ANC government moving forward into the 2020s, it is a foregone conclusion

---

[59] Mafeje, A. 1971. *The Ideology of Tribalism. The Journal of Modern African Studies,* 9(2):253-26. Cambridge University Press.

[60] Ibid.

[61] Ibid.

that the chiefs will be a major instrument in the implementation of such policy. In other words, the institution of tribalism will be used to continue to obscure and perpetuate the real nature of power relations in this country.

The more things change, the more they stay the same.

Postscript

What do I say to wind up and update this story? Writing about our beloved country is not an enjoyable and fulfilling exercise. The story is not good. By all accounts, the country is in bad shape. Apparently, it has not been able to cast off its imperialist/colonialist curse – or has it? To make matters worse, our proud new South Africa has been plagued by a host of troubles, many self-inflicted.

We have apparently gone astray from the path of liberation. Having lost our way, we are helplessly floundering in the desert, misled by the unprincipled, the unscrupulous, the self-centred and narrow-minded. The essential attributes of honesty, uprightness, integrity and a sense of honour are missing in our public life.

For many of us, current revelations have been an eye-opener. The country is mired in a morass of shameless greed and rampant corruption. In all of this, the biggest culprit has been the African National Congress (ANC), the ruling party. The country has been brought to its knees and is desperately struggling to keep its head above water.

Unfortunately, the ruling party and many others do not seem to be aware that the country is in crisis. We have reached the moment when, in the words of former US president Richard Nixon, "We must make an agonising reappraisal."

The calamity has not come about suddenly. From as early as the late 1990s, during the "Zuma for president!" campaign, there were signs that many had lost their way. The standard bearer and chief praise singer, Julius Malema, was proudly vowing his "readiness to die for Zuma". Despite the startling revelations of corruption in the Schabir Shaik trial, he defiantly asserted, "Guilty or not guilty, we want Zuma for president."

The sorry tale of the ANC's complicity in Zuma's wrongdoings is no secret. Up to the present, the ANC has not even once reprimanded their favourite Mtsholozi for his multifarious transgressions. Instead, they continue to give him votes of confidence – what moral bankruptcy! When Dr Makhosi Khoza bravely criticised their slavish subservience, they forced her out of the party. She had committed the unpardonable sin.

Instead of attending to the issues afflicting the country, the powers that be are engaged in a vanity fair of celebration after celebration, extolling the virtues of countless ANC leaders. We are treated throughout the year to a nauseating chorus of self-congratulation and ANC achievements, viz, "sacrifices in the struggle", "liberating the country", "defeating apartheid", etc.

The monotonous theme of these sermons is that we are beholden to them and, therefore, must gladly suffer their sins of commission and omission. If we are unhappy or discontented, we must not forget apartheid was far worse. Talk of poor service delivery and corruption is disloyalty. They can do no wrong.

In this undignified scramble to feed at the trough of self-enrichment, we have forgotten the urgent and vital task of building a nation. What South Africans seem to have forgotten is that the Convention for a Democratic South Africa (CODESA) and the Kempton Park Accord was meant to be the start of a process of dismantling the old South Africa and the building of a new just society.

CODESA and the Kempton Park Accord left the most important and vital question of land restitution unresolved. South Africa is a queer and bizarre country. Throughout the era of imperialist invasion and colonisation, the Dutch and British conquerors never sat down with the indigenous people, the conquered, to agree and sign a peace treaty.

The victors cynically and unilaterally used means like ethnic cleansing to uproot and displace the natives. There is not a shred of legitimacy in the way the Africans were dispossessed. The victors then cynically and brutally imposed their will and laws. It was only in the last decade of the 20th century that they finally, grudgingly, sat down with the Black majority.

They had not been converted to the idea of a single, non-racial and democratic South Africa.

They still wanted to retain as much as they could of their former exclusive rights and privileges of the old South Africa. The salient features of the old were White supremacy and Black subordination, premised on Black dispossession and no citizenship rights. They yielded on the issue of a single South African nation with universal adult franchise.

They refused to budge on the question of land restitution and that was left unresolved. The meeting at Kempton Park was not composed of victors and vanquished. Land had been taken from the Africans by force. There was blood and tears. If White

South Africans refuse to part with their ill-gotten gains, force might well be used. It will not be revenge, but do not expect smiles and handshakes.

Land restitution is not an option. It is a prerequisite and a sine qua non for a truly new South Africa. The majority are poor and dependent on government grants.

We have let these poor people down. "Old" South Africa robbed them of their land and means of livelihood. They also lost their independence, dignity and self-respect. We do not seem to realise the urgency, but time is not on our side. We must bite the bullet and not leave the problem unresolved. Posterity will have enough worries.

Our procrastination and prevarication are proof of our cowardice. Dereliction of duty is an unpardonable sin. There are clear signs that the masses are growing tired of waiting. There have already been instances of sporadic and desperate acts of land grabbing. If we keep on shilly-shallying and dilly-dallying, we will have failed in our duty. Posterity will curse us.

Throughout Xhosaland (the current Eastern Cape), the situation is desperate. This former home of heroes is in shambles. It is South Africa's Cinderella province. For years now, it has been a miserable tail-ender in everything. A complete change in the lifestyle of the inhabitants has occurred. Not long ago, one could correctly describe the inhabitants as subsistence farmers or peasants. They were dependent for their livelihood on their livestock (cattle, goats and sheep). They used their arable land to raise crops of maize, corn (amazimba), beans, pumpkins, etc.

As if by magic, that is no more. The cattle have disappeared and the lands are lying fallow. All agricultural activity has ceased, making a confounded situation worse. People ask a pertinent question: If people cannot profitably use the land they have, what would be the purpose of giving them more land?

The territory has become overpopulated and flooded with people who are neither livestock owners nor title-holders of residential sites and/or arable land. Unemployed, they have become a danger and a nuisance. Who is to blame for this impasse? It has become fashionable to blame the government for everything. In this case, we should be the last to point the finger of blame at someone else. The present government did not create this mess and, yes, the wretched fools neither worry nor care. We must accept some of the blame. We have failed to present to the government a plan of redemption. They know nothing and do not care.

In the olden days. the burden of tilling the land was borne by women. When commercial farming supervened, the ox was used and men took over from women-folk. Overpopulation has resulted in the denudation of pasturage because of the daily allotment of new households. We have failed to make the transition to mechanised farming, that is, from using oxen to using tractors instead.

For our small arable lots, we have to form cooperatives to purchase agricultural implements. We should have presented a blueprint to government. They do not take any initiative and what do they know and what do they care?

In the old South Africa, there was the Maize Board to supervise production and marketing, but the "Native areas" were excluded. The present government must bear the blame for failing to bring us under the Maize Board umbrella. Instead of taking the matter up nationally and provincially, it is preoccupied with tiny party and parochial ventures.

The whole of Xhosaland has become a depressed area, in spite of its undeniable agricultural potential. The time for talking is over. South Africa is hungry and must use the available land for production. We can become one of the world's biggest food producers and Xhosaland can become a beehive of activity. Let us wake up!

This is a vast area with enough arable land to feed the whole of southern Africa if properly used. It is criminal to allow land to be fallow.

Another shameful page in the ANC's abominable track record is their handling of Mcebesi Jonas's exposure of Gupta impropriety and presumptuousness. Mcebesi Jonas was not treated as an honourable and courageous comrade. He became something of an outcast. Gwede Mantashe's handling of the commission he headed did not enhance his reputation. It was a commission whose sole purpose was to obfuscate and bury the truth.

Everything he did could not hide the fact that he was not trying to uncover any wrongdoing. The whole exercise was a charade. We had always thought Gwede Mantashe had an independent mind. After seeing him engaged in this silly and clumsy pretence, we woke up to the reality of his readiness to do J.G. Zuma's dirty work.

It was to be the indefatigable and unthanked Thuli Madonsela who would expose the Gupta/Zuma depravity.

One would have thought the ANC – both leadership and membership – would have been aghast and perturbed. However, they remain self-satisfied and smug and make no serious attempts to self-correct. It is apparent that they have not woken up to the gravity of the situation. After all, they have got their struggle credentials and there is no formidable opposition.

Some analysts say the old organisation is rotten to the core and beyond redemption. In my view, it is evident that the ANC has outlived its usefulness and is now an encumbrance. It is aiding and abetting wrongdoers and criminals. Although it is in power and in control of the arms of the law, it is now the Democratic Alliance (DA) and the media who expose and ferret out law breakers. The ANC does not seem to know its duty anymore.

Remember the way its MPs zealously and maliciously obstructed and frustrated former public protector, Thuli Madonsela? It was painful to watch. You would have thought she was the enemy and not the incumbent head of a state organ they were obliged to support. They were an absolute disgrace.

Convocation medal to Mthatha law doyen

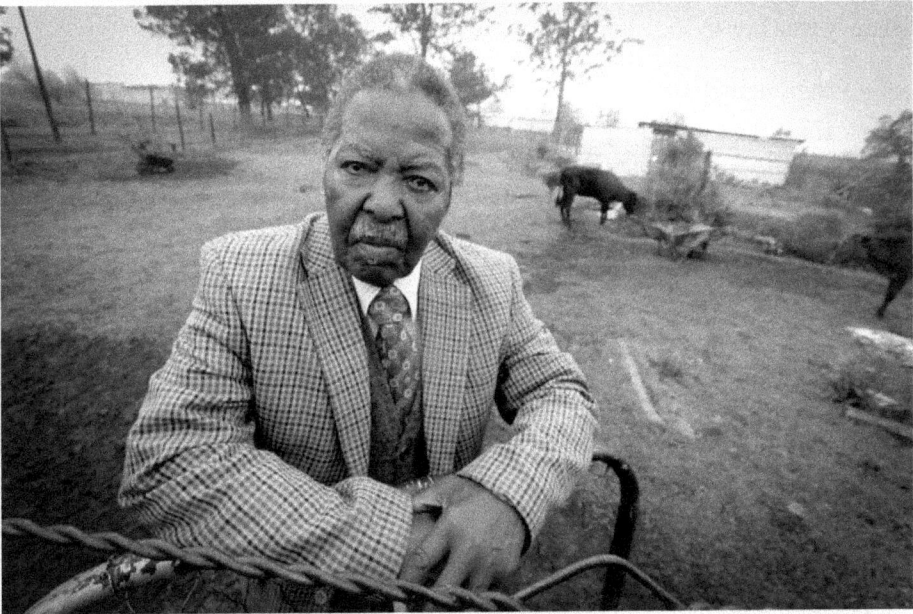

Law alumnus Mda Mda, this year's recipient of the President of Convocation Medal, photographed at his home near Mthatha. Past medal recipients include Dr Kate Philip, Dr Richard (Dick) van der Ross, Anne Templeton, Professor Wiseman Nkuhlu, Justice MM Corbett, and Sir Aaron Klug.

Retired Mthatha attorney Mda Mda, who enrolled for a law degree at UCT in 1944, is this year's recipient of the President of Convocation Medal, awarded annually to an alumnus who has contributed to the common good.

At 92, Mda Mda has a memory like an elephant.

He remembers the upset over Mussolini's 1935 invasion of Abyssinia, Africa's last 'free country', as the year is still pegged in his mind.

He was a grade 7 pupil at Lovedale College (whose famous alumni include Steve Biko, Z.K. Matthews, Govan Mbeki, Tiyo Soga, Charles Nqakula and King Sobhuza II) and about to embark on the last phase of his schooling.

He'd had "the very good fortune" of being born to Simeon and Leah (nèe Mzimba) in the rural village of Ncambedlana, near Mthatha – both good scholars and from whom he no doubt inherited his attentive and enquiring mind.

Mda matriculated from Lovedale in 1940 and recalls those formative years keenly, particularly a young English teacher who infused a love of history in the young Mda. He was deeply disappointed when she returned to Britain because of the war.

"History was my special delight," he says.

In 1941 Mda signed up for a BA with majors in history and native administration at Fort Hare. The formality of university life surprised him; here he was called "Mr Mda", academic excellence was "number one", a residence curfew of 8 p.m. was strictly enforced, and there was no intoxicating drink allowed. Neither was there any politics on campus.

"I left Fort Hare politically illiterate," he says.

But by the time Mda graduated in 1943, he had been afforded another gift: the discovery of books and the thrill of "delving deeply" into the library.

"I was particularly interested in imperialist and colonial laws."

Legal routes

However, the young Mda, who practised as an attorney for some 49 years, almost missed out on a legal career.

After graduating from Fort Hare he completed a diploma in education to become a teacher. But his father persuaded him to take up law instead.

To do so he travelled south to UCT and enrolled in the law faculty for an LLB degree in 1944.

But because of the length and structure of the degree and personal circumstances, he was unable to complete this qualification at UCT.

He was living in Langa at the time and classes were held at the old Union House in Queen Victoria Street in town. Travelling via tram and train had become a burden and he was also acutely aware of being a drain on his father's resources.

He later moved to student lodgings in District Six, hoping to study part-time while teaching in Langa.

"It was not easy," he says. "I had to write home frequently for money. I felt it was selfish to take another degree."

And while he later persuaded a Fort Hare lecturer to allow him to do non-degree law courses through that institution, he realised his dream of becoming an advocate was vanishing.

Nonetheless, two years later Mda persuaded local Mthatha firm Gush Muggleston & Heathcore to take him on as an articled clerk. It was an unsatisfactory experience. He shared the 'native office' with an interpreter and a messenger.

"I had no access to the library and I was not taught anything."

But he did manage to pass articles. And so after six years Mda left the firm to start practising as an attorney in Mqanduli, a small town nearby.

If his route to law had been complicated, starting a practice was unnerving.

"I'd never been given a single case. I'd never been in a court, I'd never seen a Supreme Court summons and I had to pass the attorney's admission exams. I resorted to the library. And because of what I'd learnt in my time at UCT, I was able to pass that easily."

In his personal life things were changing too. In 1954 Mda married Dorothy, a teacher in Mthatha, and they had five daughters and a son, the last-born.

Early political alliance

Although Mda had come out of Fort Hare politically illiterate, one of the pivotal events in the early years of his career was his involvement in 1944 in the Non-European Unity Movement (NEUM). The development was to shape his thinking, political beliefs and actions.

Chroniclers of South African history have perhaps consigned the NEUM, which had been launched in 1943, to a dusty shelf in the annals. Made up of members who were teachers, writers, and intellectuals, the NEUM made a significant, if not forgotten, contribution to the country's liberation struggle.

It was the first organisation in South Africa to adopt non-racialism, rejecting the notion of different human races and African 'inferiority' propounded under apartheid. The movement was also committed to non-collaboration with the apartheid government.

In fact, NEUM's ten-point programme preceded the ANC's Freedom Charter by 12 years.

"Many believed the Freedom Charter was an imitation of the ten-point programme," said Mda.

The movement had put out a declaration after the first Nationalist government was voted in: "It was something like: 'We, the people of Transkei reject the nefarious policy of apartheid'," he says. "There were no dissensions. We spoke with one voice.

"We had decided that the government must be told that we in the Transkei rejected this policy. We sent delegates to Pretoria as representatives of the Native Representative Council. Pretoria was shocked at these tame and compliant natives of the Transkei delivering this ultimatum."

But the ultimatum had other consequences. It was the start, says Mda, of a "new breed of civil servants" – information officers appointed to be part of the propaganda machine.

Life after law

Mda's long legal career was centred on criminal and native law. He practised as an attorney until his retirement in 2001. But even at 92, he remains active in the law fraternity as an advisor and mentor and a well-respected member of his community.

"I've become an armchair theorist and critic," he quips, preferring instead the rewards of keeping cattle and growing vegetables at the home he shares with his daughter near Mthatha.

"This Xhosa boy likes cattle and the garden," he says, lamenting the scarcity of rain in the Eastern Cape. This morning, the heat has driven him indoors.

Given his many years, Mda is philosophical: "The heart wants to do these things, but where is the strength?"

Mda will turn 93 on 25 March next year. A love of books ("With my books, I never experienced solitude") has accompanied him tenderly into his latter years, "though I received so many on my 90th birthday, I'm still trying to get through them all!"

He was last in the Mother City in June this year, for his eldest daughter's 60th birthday, and looks forward to returning to UCT this month to revive old memories. It will be graduation season (truncated after the rescheduling of exams following a gritty period of student protest); a time of victory and celebration.

But Mda has a message for the students.

"I'd like our youth to be more serious. There is so much that needs to be done in South Africa because of the legacy of the past. It behoves us to do a lot of cleaning up of the Augean Stables of apartheid.

"And there is much to be done to recover the lost years. It's a heavy burden for this generation."

He pauses to reflect. "Everything is upside down."

15 December 2015
Story by Helen Swingler. Photo by Lulamile Feni
Available from https://bit.ly/2HdnXSz

www.ingramcontent.com/pod-product-compliance
Lightning Source LLC
Chambersburg PA
CBHW080403270326
41927CB00015B/3335